QUOTABLE SAINTS

Quotable Saints

Compiled by
Ronda De Sola Chervin

Servant Publications
Ann Arbor, Michigan

Scripture texts in this work are taken from the New American Bible
with Revised New Testament, © 1986 Confraternity of Christian
Doctrine. All rights reserved. The texts from the Old Testament are
taken from the New American Bible, © 1970 Confraternity of
Christian Doctrine. All rights reserved. No part of the New
American Bible with Revised New Testament may be reproduced
without permission in writing from the copyright owner.

Published by Servant Publications
P.O. Box 8617
Ann Arbor, Michigan 48107

Acknowledgments are listed in the last appendix.

Cover design by Michael Andaloro.
Cover painting courtesy of Art Resource, New York.
Detail from Gentile da Fabriano, Polyptych. Brera, Pinacoteca.

92 93 94 95 96 10 9 8 7 6 5 4 3 2

Printed in the United States of America
ISBN 0-89283-733-0

Library of Congress Cataloging-in-Publication Data

Quotable saints / compiled by Ronda De Sola Chervin.
    p. cm.
  Includes bibliographical references and indexes.
  ISBN 0-89283-733-0
  1. Spiritual life—Catholic authors—Quotations, maxims, etc.
2. Christian saints—Quotations.   I. Chervin, Ronda.
BX2350.2.Q66   1992
242'.2——dc20   91-41517

Contents

Introduction

WHY READ QUOTES OF THE SAINTS? Isn't it better to concentrate on Scripture, the Word of God? Studying the wisdom of the saints has long been a tradition in the church. I believe this is mainly because these forerunners of the faith have already victoriously traveled the same path we are trying to follow.

Deemed worthy of veneration after an often lengthy investigation, the saints are the heroes and heroines of spirituality whom the church has judged to have been taken immediately after death into the bosom of God. There they adore the Father and intercede for us. The reality of their sanctity, therefore, gives much greater credibility to their words of wisdom than we would accord the beautiful thoughts of others which might be dismissed as mere idealism.

Here are a few examples. Does the famous saying, "Our hearts are restless until they rest in thee," take on added weight when we learn that it was coined by St. Augustine, a restless youth who converted at age thirty-three? As a young man snared by sexual sin and involved in a religious cult, he eventually came to realize that only the true God could satisfy the deepest longings of his heart. After his conversion, he even lived for many years as a faithful celibate and was a staunch defender of orthodoxy.

Does the statement, "Let nothing disturb thee," ring differently when we realize it was penned by St. Teresa of Avila? This renowned mystic was not a quiet contemplative but a courageous advocate of spiritual renewal and reform during a tumultuous age of church history. In particular, she found herself embroiled in many difficult legal disputes when trying to establish new foundations for her order.

In dividing the quotations from the saints into categories, I thought that a different and helpful approach would be to see these gems of truth in the context of our own longing to move from a negative state of mind or heart to a positive one—from sadness to joy and from despair to hope, for example. Such chapter headings indicate my own conviction that the Holy Spirit can make use of the faith-filled wisdom of the saints to overcome the confusion and doubt that comes with negativity. Once we become convinced of the direction God wants us to take, we are more ready to pray for relief from emotions and problems that weigh us down.

This book is intended for two types of readers. One is the popular reader who is inspired by the spirituality of the saints and may want to use this book in daily devotions—perhaps by following certain themes. The second is pastors, teachers, ministers, counselors, and others who may find the topical arrangement of quotes helpful for homilies, talks, and workshops, and in guiding others in spiritual direction.

A question may arise as you proceed in your spiritual reading of *Quotable Saints*. How do you know that a particular thought is right for you in your present situation? Such an uncertainty can be especially disconcerting when your problem is painful and when the solution proposed by one saint seems to contradict what is recommended by another!

To decide if the message of a particular quotation is meant for your life, ask the Holy Spirit to show you through personal prayer, sharing with mature Christian friends, or asking a mentor. In our tradition of Christian growth, it is never advisable to try to walk on the path with only ideas as guides. If you do not already have one, perhaps God wants to lead you to a worthy spiritual director who can help you to know what general precepts to apply in your own life.

Let me explain the designations given to the authors of the quotations herein. The title *Servant of God* is given to deceased Catholics undergoing the process of canonization because so many considered them to be holy during their lifetime. *Venerable* is a title given to a servant of God by the Sacred Congregation for the Causes of the Saints, with the approval of the Holy Father, when this person has exhibited heroic virtue during his or her life on earth.

Such a venerable individual may be called *blessed* after miracles during life and after death have been studied and approved (the process of beatification). Canonization depends upon a miracle occurring after beatification has been approved by the pope. Only after beatification may an individual Catholic be publicly venerated. After full canonization, the word *saint* can be used.

In this book of quotations, I have followed the example of many other such collections by choosing primarily writings of the blessed and the canonized saints. But I have also included venerables and servants of God, especially in cases where beatification is widely predicted within our lifetimes. In order to achieve a better balance, I have tried to include more than the usual number of quotations from women saints. I also balance the writings of the more famous Western saints with those from the Eastern traditions associated with Greek, Middle-Eastern, and Russian spirituality. I hope that these selections will help you appreciate more of the feminine side of spirituality and the spiritual riches of our brothers and sisters from Eastern traditions, especially in worship and mysticism.

Often in my own spiritual journey, quotations from the saints have been of great influence. Mourning the death of a friend, I think of St. Elizabeth Seton's famous line: "In heaven we will know each other by the glance of the soul." In times of indignation over the smugness of someone who is ignorant of the faith, I remember the saying of St. Francis de Sales: "You can win more converts with a spoonful of honey than a barrelful of vinegar." Or in times of near despair, I am comforted by the wisdom of Blessed Julian of Norwich, "All shall be well, and all shall be well, and all manner of things shall be well." I hope that *Quotable Saints* may provide similar help on your pilgrimage.

1

Ambition to Contentment

I N OUR SOCIETY SUCCESS IS CONSIDERED by many to be the main goal in life. In business courses in some Catholic colleges, students are even advised to throw out the catechism, so they can rush ahead without being held back by old-fashioned ethical concerns! It is usually when symptoms of stress overtake the harried yuppie of our day that questioning begins about the merits of such a goal. Is ambition really the ultimate good in life? Or are other things more important?

Christian teaching, while never condemning success in the pursuit of the good, tells us, "Seek first the kingdom of heaven and its justice, and all things shall be added unto you" (Mt 6:33). We ought to hope that God will use all the talent he has given us in letting us be instruments in our good works, but we should leave success in his hands and flee from decisions that involve seeking success at all costs. For many, this might mean refusing promotions that involve so much overtime as to detract from a healthy family life. For others this might mean leaving behind lucrative employment to live in a more wholesome environment where Christian support is more available.

The lives of the saints are studded with examples of blessed failure. St. Catherine of Alexandria, a theologian and rhetorician, was rewarded for her successful public debate with pagan philosophers by being tortured and executed on a wheel of fire. St. Elizabeth of Hungary, entitled to the life of a queen, is found instead nursing the poor as a Third Order Franciscan. St. Ignatius Loyola, forced to abandon courtly military life when wounded in battle, becomes another kind of courtier as the leader of men dedicated to the Lord alone. St. Benedict Joseph Labré, turned away from the contemplative orders he longed to join, ended up living the life of a street person in the alleys of Rome.

✠ ✠ ✠

The honors of this world, what are they but puff, and emptiness and peril of falling? **St. Augustine**

Christ tells us that if we want to join him, we shall travel the way he took. It is surely not right that the Son of God should go his way on the path of shame while the sons of men walk the way of worldly honor.

St. John of Avila

Oh how insinuating and imperceptible is the passion of pleasing men: it possesses even the wise! For the effects of other passions are easily seen by those who obey them and so bring those they possess to humility and mourning. But the effort to please men clothes itself in the words and appearances of piety, so that men whom it beguiles find it hard to detect its various aspects.

St. Mark the Ascetic

What men call fame is, after all, but a very windy thing. A man thinks that many are praising him, and talking of him alone, and yet they spend but a very small part of the day thinking of him, being occupied with things of their own. **St. Thomas More**

Do not seek to be regarded as somebody, don't compare yourself to others in anything. Leave the world, mount the cross, discard all earthly things, shake the dust from off your feet. **St. Barsanuphius**

The saints were so completely dead to themselves that they cared very little whether others agreed with them or not. **St. John Vianney**

Ambition is the mother of hypocrisy and prefers to skulk in corners and dark places. It cannot endure the light of day. It is an unclean vice wallowing in the depths, always hidden, but with ever an eye to advancement. **St. Bernard**

I have always been content here.... I would rather by the divine mercy be the least among the Passionists than be the son of the king and heir to the kingdom.

St. Gabriel Possenti

We crush the head of the serpent when we scorn and trample underfoot the glory of the world, the praises, the vanities and all the other pomps of pride.

Blessed Marie of the Incarnation

Those who covet honour, I mean a great name, really covet no substantial thing at all.

Venerable John Henry Cardinal Newman

You are ambitious: for knowledge?... for leadership?... for great ventures? Good, very good. But let it be for Christ, for love. **Venerable José Escriva**

In those around you, you don't see brothers; you see stepping stones. **Venerable José Escriva**

2

Anger to Peacefulness

UNCONTROLLED AND BITTER ANGER has always been considered a vice among Christians. In our era it has assumed even more serious proportions due to increases in violent crime: wife battering, assault, rape, incest, murder, to name a few. We are not to let the sun set on our anger, not only because we are to dwell in loving harmony whenever possible, but also because such anger can grow to intense hatred leading to breakup of families, gang feuds, war between nations, and to rebellion against even God himself.

In his *Summa Theologica*, St. Thomas Aquinas distinguishes between righteous anger about injustice in the world and our own legitimate rights, and wrongful anger. It is a sin to let evil reign without protest! About such matters we are right to be assertive. On the other hand, Thomas comes down heavily on anger that is out of proportion—that is cold, vicious, vengeful. This kind of anger we must pray against and confess before it takes root in our hearts.

I believe that we also have to watch a chronic irritation symptomatic of our refusal to put up with the sufferings God allows us to endure. Sometimes humor can come to our aid as an antidote to taking ourselves so seriously that everything that stands in our way causes fits of anger.

A good example of humor overcoming legitimate anger can be found in the life of Aquinas himself. It is said that his confreres in the Dominican Order liked to ridicule him for his absorption in philosophical problems and his scrupulous obedience. "Thomas, Thomas," one cried out, "Come, look out the window. A cow is jumping over the moon!" The portly theologian left his work and rushed to see the prodigy. When the assembled friars laughed at him, he replied, "I would rather believe that a cow was jumping over the moon than that a Dominican would tell a lie!"

More seriously, St. Gerard Majella was once accused of seducing a penitent! As he had taken a vow never to defend himself, he allowed himself to be reviled for this supposed sin, never giving into anger for this wrong. Finally, he was totally exonerated, and then revered for the way he had turned the other cheek.

✠ ✠ ✠

Anger is a kind of temporary madness. St. Basil

Guard your tongue when your husband is angry.
St. Monica

Belligerents are not reluctant to have peace, but they want a peace to their own liking. St. Augustine

Peace is the tranquillity of order. St. Augustine

Tell me, how are we two going to face the Day of Judgement? The sun is witness that it has gone down on our anger not one day but for many a long year.... St. Jerome

The mind that has forgotten true knowledge wages war with people for things that are harmful to it, as though they were profitable. St. Mark the Ascetic

If a man cannot bear being reviled, he will not see glory. If he is not cleansed of gall, he will not savor sweetness. St. Barsanuphius

Argument is a fishing line baited with veracity (defense of truth, self-justification, self-defense) by which we are seduced into swallowing the hook of sin. In this manner, hooked by tongue and throat, the poor soul is wont to be ravished by evil spirits.

St. Simeon the New Theologian

In order to avoid discord, never contradict anyone except in case of sin or some danger to a neighbor.

St. Louis IX (King of France)

The world would have peace if the men of politics would only follow the Gospels. St. Birgitta of Sweden

Anger is tamed and becomes transformed into benevolence only through courage and mercy; for these destroy the enemies that besiege the city of the soul—the first, the enemies outside and the second, those within. St. Gregory of Sinai

There is no sin nor wrong that gives a man such a fore-taste of hell in this life as anger and impatience.

O lovely compassion. You are the balm that snuffs out rage and cruelty in the soul. This compassion, compassionate Father, I beg you to give to all.

Not by violence will [the Church] regain her beauty but through peace and through the constant and humble prayers and sweat and tears poured out with eager desire. **St. Catherine of Siena**

Maintain a spirit of peace and you'll save a thousand souls. **St. Seraphim of Sarov**

You will effect more by kind words and a courteous manner, than by anger or sharp rebuke, which should never be used but in necessity. **St. Angela Merici**

Dismiss all anger and look into yourself a little. Remember that he of whom you are speaking is your brother, and, as he is in the way of salvation, God can make him a saint, in spite of his present weakness.

St. Thomas of Villanova

Peace and union are the most necessary of all things for men who live in common, and nothing serves so well to establish and maintain them as the forebearing charity whereby we put up with another's defects. There is no one who has not his faults, and who is not in some way a burden to others, whether he be a superior or a subject, an old man or a young, a scholar or a dunce. **St. Robert Bellarmine**

A man given to fasting thinks himself very devout if he fasts, although his heart may be filled with hatred.

Much concerned with sobriety, he does not dare to wet his tongue with wine or even water but won't hesitate to drink deep of his neighbor's blood by detraction and calumny. **St. Francis de Sales**

The way to overcome the devil when he excites feelings of hatred for those who injure us is immediately to pray for their conversion. **St. John Vianney**

It is easier to become angry than to restrain oneself and easier to threaten a boy than to persuade him. It is more fitting to be persistent in punishing our own impatience and pride than to correct the boys.

St. John Bosco

Why lose your temper if by doing so you offend God, annoy other people, give yourself a bad time... and have to find it again in the end. **Venerable José Escriva**

3

Annoyance to Patience

PATIENCE IS SO IMPORTANT a virtue because it is impossible in an imperfect world to live without it! Those who meet every annoyance with impatience either stud their everyday conversation with curse words or boil with inner rage.

In a fallen world, everything we long for comes more slowly than we would wish, with delay seeming to promise disaster. Sören Kierkegaard, the acclaimed Danish Lutheran theologian, used to say that impatience was at the root of all sin! For example, impatience in not having found a spouse can be at the root of grabbing an available person for casual sex!

Instead, Scripture admonishes us to imitate those who "through faith and patience inherit the promises" (Heb 6:12). It is incredible to read about the patience of the saints. Think of Blessed Marie of the Incarnation in the wilds of Canada watching the convent she had built with such difficulty burn down within a few hours. Instead of giving up, she quietly offered up this sacrifice and began rebuilding. Far from getting annoyed and discouraged when put into chains and placed under house arrest, St. Paul continued his preaching, starting with his jailers!

✠ ✠ ✠

Patient endurance is the perfection of charity.

St. Ambrose

To live with patience and die with delight. **St. Augustine**

It is a common experience even among patient people that at the moment when they suffer, they are not affected by any vexation.... But when after a time they recall what they have suffered, they become inflamed with resentment and seek out reasons for revenge.

St. Gregory the Great

Let your understanding strengthen your patience. In serenity look forward to the joy that follows sadness.

St. Peter Damian

Patience is not good if when you may be free you allow yourself to become a slave. **St. Bernard**

St. Francis de Sales, that great saint, would leave off writing with the letter of a word half-formed in order to reply to an interruption. **St. John Vianney**

Then I was transformed and left to myself in depression, weary of my life and irked with myself, so that I kept the patience to go on living only with difficulty...

and immediately after this Our Lord again gave me comfort and rest of soul in delight and certitude.

Blessed Julian of Norwich

He did submit himself unto the elements, unto cold and heat, hunger and thirst... concealing his power and despoiling himself thereof in the likeness of man, in order that he might teach us weak and wretched mortals with what patience we ought to bear tribulation. **Blessed Angela of Foligno**

O religious soul, dove beloved of Christ, behold those little pieces of straw which the world tramples under its feet. They are the virtues practiced by the Saviour and thy Spouse, for which He Himself has set thee an example: humility, meekness, poverty, penance, patience, and mortification. **St. Anthony of Padua**

True, the people of the world do not offer me [God] glory in the way they ought, by loving me above all things. But my mercy and charity are reflected in this, because I lend them time and do not order the earth to swallow them up for their sins. No,... I order the earth to give them a share of its fruits.

St. Catherine of Siena

There is no such thing as bad weather. All weather is good because it is God's. **St. Teresa of Avila**

Whenever anything disagreeable or displeasing happens to you, remember Christ crucified and be silent.

St. John of the Cross

Without the burden of afflictions it is impossible to reach the height of grace. The gifts of grace increase as the struggles increase. **St. Rose of Lima**

Many would be willing to have afflictions provided that they be not inconvenienced by them.

When you encounter difficulties and contradictions, do not try to break them, but bend them with gentleness and time.

Have patience with all the world, but first of all with yourself.

Suffer and offer up those trifling injuries, those petty inconveniences, that daily befall you. This toothache, this headache, this cold, this contempt or scorn.

The state of marriage is one that requires more virtue and constancy than any other. It is a perpetual exercise in mortification. **St. Francis de Sales**

The prayer of a sick person is his patience and his acceptance of the sickness for the love of Jesus Christ.

St. Charles of Sezze

Do as the storekeeper does with his merchandise; make a profit on every article. Suffer not the loss of the tiniest fragment of the true cross. It may only be the sting of a fly or the point of a pin that annoys you; it may be the little eccentricities of a neighbor, some unintentional slight, the insignificant loss of a penny, some little restlessness of soul, a light pain in your limbs. Make a profit on every article as the grocer does, and you will soon be wealthy in God. **St. Louis Marie de Montfort**

My precious children stick to me like little burrs, they are so fearful of losing me again [after a trip]. The moment I shake one off one side another clings on the opposite, nor can I write one word without some sweet interruption. St. Elizabeth Seton

Restraining my impatience cost me so much that I was bathed in perspiration. St. Thérèse of Lisieux

You should bear patiently the bad temper of other people, the slights, the rudeness that may be offered you. St. John Bosco

Never rebuke while you are still indignant about a fault committed—wait until the next day, or even longer. And then, calmly, and with a purer intention, make your reprimand. You will gain more by a friendly word than by a three hour quarrel. Venerable José Escriva

4

Bewilderment to Trust

IN OUR SOCIETY TODAY relationships often cause more wounding than stability. As a result it is hard to trust in others or even in God. We are bewildered and expect the worst when trouble strikes.

Trust has always been a hard-won virtue. The saints follow the Scripture in having recourse in trouble to "the good shepherd" (Ps 23:1). God merits our unwavering trust.

Think of St. Frances Cabrini of Italy. She was terrified of the sea, taking her life in her hands to obey the pope who wanted a band of Sisters to cross the Atlantic and minister to the Italian immigrants in America who were losing their faith in a land where few spoke their tongue. Think of the Asian and African martyrs, in countries so young to the faith, who were tortured to death so greatly did they trust in the Lord. Let us listen to the calming words of the saints about bringing our mistrust and bewilderment to the Lord.

✠ ✠ ✠

Receive the accidents that befall thee as good, knowing that nothing happens without God.

Teachings of the Twelve Apostles

On the way to her martyrdom:
We are not in our own power, but in the power of God.

St. Perpetua

You will lose nothing of what you have renounced for the Lord, for in its own time it will return to you manifold. **St. Mark the Ascetic**

God measures out affliction to our need.

St. John Chrysostom

One and the same violence of affliction proves, purifies and melts the good, and condemns, wastes and casts out the bad. **St. Augustine**

Let us not esteem worldly prosperity or adversity as things real or of any moment, but let us live elsewhere, and raise all our attention to Heaven; esteeming sin as the only true evil, and nothing truly good but virtue which unites us to God. **St. Gregory Nazianzen**

While the ship is at sea, it is a prey to dangers and winds. When it reaches a calm and peaceful harbour, it no longer fears dangers, calamities of the winds, but remains safe. In the same way, while you are among men you must expect tribulation, dangers and mental buffetings. But when you reach the harbour of silence prepared for you, then you will have no fear. **St. Barsanuphius**

All shall be well, and all shall be well, and all manner of things shall be well. **Blessed Julian of Norwich**

If God causes you to suffer much, it is a sign that He has great designs for you, and that He certainly intends to make you a saint. St. Ignatius Loyola

Comfort in tribulation can be secured only on the sure ground of faith holding as true the words of Scripture and the teaching of the Catholic Church. St. Thomas More

Those who call to mind the sufferings of Christ and who offer up their own to God through His passion find their pains sweet and pleasant. St. Mary Magdalene dei Pazzi

The purest suffering bears and carries in its train the purest understanding. St. John of the Cross

Let nothing disturb thee,
nothing affright thee;
all things are passing;
God never changeth;
Patient endurance
attaineth to all things;
who God possesseth
in nothing is wanting
alone God sufficeth. St. Teresa of Avila

It is not enough to be afflicted because God wills it; but we must be so as He wills it, when He wills it, for as long as He wills it, and exactly in the manner in which it pleases Him.

Make sickness itself a prayer. St. Francis de Sales

Surely nothing is too much for Him when there is question of sanctifying a soul. He hands over the body and soul to weakness in order to purify them in contempt of earthly things and in the love of His Majesty. He wounds and He heals them; He crucifies them on His cross in order to glorify them in His glory; in brief He gives them death in order to have them live in eternity. Let us accept these appearances of evil in order to have the real goods they produce, and we shall be happy both in this life and in the next. **St. Vincent de Paul**

Blessed Marie of the Incarnation had left her son with the extended family when she was convinced God wanted her to enter the convent:
My dear and beloved son. All this year I have been in great torment imagining the pitfalls where you might stumble, but finally our gracious God gave me peace in the belief that his loving and fatherly goodness would never lose what had been abandoned for his love.... I have never loved you except in the poverty of Jesus Christ in whom I have found all riches... not a day passes that I don't offer you to his love.... I speak of you ceaselessly to Jesus, Mary and Joseph.
Blessed Marie of the Incarnation

Unexpected blows, at the moment they fall, sometimes stun those who receive them and fling them into trouble which prevents them from profiting by their disgrace for the time being. But be a little patient.... Without this misfortune you might not have been wholly bad, but perhaps you would not have been entirely good either.

It is a kind of death to leave a place where one is well known and has friends. **Blessed Claude de la Colombierè**

To love [God] and suffer blindly. St. Margaret Mary Alacoque

In the novitiate, I was almost always ill and so small of stature that I was unable to reach the lectern, nor could I help my fellow novices in the necessary chores of the novitiate.... However, with my profession I gained health and strength and grew to medium size. I attribute all this to my profession, for which I give infinite thanks to God. Blessed Junipero Serra

What avails melancholy forebodings, and indulgence of feeling which can never alter the event of things? One would, rather, look at life's realities as they are guided by a just and merciful Protector who orders every occurrence in its time and place. St. Elizabeth Seton

Concerning the early tragic death of her husband:
I know that these contradictory events are permitted and guided by thy wisdom, which solely is light. We are in darkness and must be thankful that our knowledge is not wanted [needed] to perfect thy work.

St. Elizabeth Seton

Say always, "My beloved and despised Redeemer, how sweet it is to suffer for you."
If you embrace all things in life as coming from the hands of God, and even embrace death to fulfill his holy will, assuredly you will die a saint. St. Alphonsus Liguori

An iron is fashioned by fire and on an anvil, so in the fire of suffering and under the weight of trials, our souls receive the form which Our Lord desires them to have.

St. Madeleine Sophie Barat

Regarding a grave illness:
He who has made me, unmakes me. **Blessed Eugénie Smet**

I will see the hand of God in all that happens to me, attributing nothing to individual people, who are but instruments used by Him in the work of our sanctification. **Blessed Raphaela Maria**

Let the crucifix be not only in my eyes and on my breast, but in my heart. **St. Bernadette**

Whatever, wherever I am, I can never be thrown away. If I am in sickness, my sickness may serve Him; in perplexity, my perplexity may serve Him; if I am in sorrow, my sorrow may serve Him.... He does nothing in vain; He may prolong my life, He may shorten it; He knows what He is about. He may take away my friends, He may throw me among strangers, He may make me feel desolate, make my spirits sink, hide the future from me— still He knows what He is about.
Venerable John Henry Cardinal Newman

Without you, my sweet Savior, I remain in darkness and grief. Without you, most gentle Lamb, I remain in worry and fear. Without you, Son of the Almighty God, I remain in confusion and shame. **Blessed John of Alverna**

I worry until midnight and from then on I let God worry. **Blessed Louis Guanella**

God sometimes allows us to be in such profound darkness that not a single star shines in our skies. The reason is that we must be reminded that we are on earth only to suffer, while following our gentle Saviour along a dark and thorny path. We are pilgrims and strangers on earth. Pilgrims sleep in tents and sometimes cross deserts, but the thought of their homeland makes them forget everything else. **Venerable Charles de Foucauld**

Thank the good God for having visited you through suffering; if we knew the value of suffering, we would ask for it. **Blessed Brother André**

So you have failed? You cannot fail. You have not failed: you have gained experience. Forward!

Venerable José Escriva

5

Complaining
to Gratitude

IN SPITE OF THE MANY BENEFITS God has blessed us with,
how many times do we complain about little difficulties and trials? We lose sight of the big picture and fail
to appreciate the really important things. Just as we
cannot benefit from a wrapped gift under a Christmas
tree until we open it, so gratitude can be seen as our
way of opening the gift of God's love intended by all
the small and big positive events in our lives.

"In all things give thanks" (Eph 5:20). We can increase our joy in daily living, as the saints did, by letting
our thoughts dwell on all that is good, especially the
promise of our final redemption and salvation. How
ashamed we feel of our own complaining ways when we
read about a saint like Blessed Margaret of Castello.
She was blind, hunchbacked, and crippled, left by her
parents to shift for herself on the steps of the church,
yet she spent her days in praise of God and service to
other unfortunates!

✠ ✠ ✠

We should not accept in silence the benefactions of God, but return thanks for them. St. Basil

Be eager for more frequent gatherings for thanksgiving to God and his glory. For when we meet thus, the forces of Satan are annulled and his destructive power is cancelled in the concord of your faith.

St. Ignatius of Antioch

... Man, God created to be a witness and grateful interpreter of His works. This is what men should strive for, lest they die as dumb animals, without having seen or understood God and His works.... When you lie down on your bed, remember with thanksgiving blessings and providence of God. Thereupon, filled with this good thought, you will rejoice in spirit and... brimming with the feeling of good, will wholeheartedly and with all strength glorify God, giving Him from the heart praises that rise on high. St. Anthony the Great

Thanking is a new, inward knowing, with great reverence and loving awe. Blessed Julian of Norwich

He that complains or murmurs is not perfect, nor is he even a good Christian. St. John of the Cross

Concerning the sick she ministered to:
If there is likeliness of illness leading to death, I will do my utmost to make them offer up acts of faith and hope and confidence... and I will try to give them some knowledge of the grandeur, beauty and love of God, and the joy of possessing Him eternally and of the glory of the blessed. St. Louise de Marillac

The blessings [God] has given me... are scorn of the world—of its pleasures, its riches, its honors; and the love of the cross, of poverty, of humility; as well as the honor of his constant presence, of familiarity and intimacy with him, and above all the love of his love.

Blessed Marie of the Incarnation

If we have any natural defect, either in mind or body, let us not grieve and be sorry for ourselves. Who is there that ever receives a gift and tries to make bargains about it? Let us, then, return thanks for what He has bestowed on us. Who can tell whether, if we had had a larger share of ability or stronger health, we should not have possessed them to our destruction.

St. Alphonsus Liguori

My spiritual life has not changed: it is filled with the presence of Our Lord, and of his beloved saints who were with Him on earth, and is one with that of those I love so much in this world. In such pleasant company the days pass quickly and I can do nothing but give thanks to God.... We should accept, as we would a favor, every moment of our lives and whatever they may bring, whether it is good or bad, but the crosses with even greater gratitude than the rest. Crosses release us from this world and by doing so bind us to God.

Venerable Charles de Foucauld

6

Confusion to Contemplation

THE BUSY RAT RACE OF MODERN LIFE tends to make our lives cluttered and confused, instead of focused and peaceful. The saints offer the more fruitful and ultimately fulfilling path of contemplation—full time for those so called and at some point during the day for those called to the active life.

In a dance-drama about Martha and Mary, my sister, Carla De Sola, vividly portrayed St. Martha in the image of the typically rushed woman of our times. In her scattered state, Martha calls out: "For whom is all this busyness? For them? For me?" Calmed by the words of the Lord, Martha can sit with Mary at the feet of Jesus enjoying the highest gifts of prayer.

Even the most active of saints loved contemplation, for what is contemplation but a foretaste of our eternal destiny of absorption in the all-beautiful one who made us for himself? But how do we enter into contemplation? By the simplest route. We have only to open ourselves often, in simple prayer of desire, allowing time for God to respond.

✠ ✠ ✠

The contemplation of God is promised to us as the goal of all our acts and the eternal consummation of all our joys. **St. Augustine**

As no darkness can be seen by anyone surrounded by light, so no trivialities can capture the attention of anyone who has his eyes on Christ. **St. Gregory of Nyssa**

When your mind, inflamed by longing for God, little by little divests itself of flesh, as it were, and turns away from all thoughts engendered by sensory impressions, or from memory, being at the same time full of adoration and rejoicing, then you may conclude that it has approached the boundaries of prayer. **St. Nilus of Sinai**

The approach to perfect prayer is when a man is freed from dispersion of thoughts and sees his mind, enlightened by the Lord, filled with joy. **St. Barsanuphius**

Merely to love things above is already to mount on high.
St. Gregory the Great

No one can approach God without withdrawing from the world. By withdrawal I do not mean change of physical dwelling place, but withdrawal from worldly affairs. The virtue of withdrawal from the world consists in not occupying your mind with the world.

If a man reads lines of great meaning without going deeply into them, his heart remains poor; and the holy force which, through wondrous understanding of the soul, gives most sweet food to the heart, grows dim in him.

Prayer is one thing, and contemplation in prayer is another.... Prayer is sowing, contemplation the reaping of the harvest, when the reaper is filled with wonder at the ineffable sight of the beautiful ears of corn, which have sprung up before him from the little naked seeds that he sowed. St. Isaak of Syria

When, urged by love, the mind soars to God, it has no sensation either of itself or of anything existing. Illumined by the limitless Divine light, it is insensible to all the created, just as is the physical eye to stars in the light of the sun.

Blessed is the mind which, passing by all creatures, constantly rejoices in God's Beauty.

By means of pure prayer the soul escapes completely from the midst of creatures, carried to God, as it were, on wings. St. Maximus the Confessor

The grace of contemplation is granted only in response to a longing and importunate desire. St. Bernard

What a veil is for the eyes, so worldly thoughts and life recollections are for the mind, or the eye of the soul. So long as we allow them to exist we shall see nothing; but when we banish them through memory of death, we shall see the true light which illumines every man that comes into the world. St. Simeon the New Theologian

Our labor here is brief, but the reward is eternal. Do not be disturbed by the clamor of the world which passes like a shadow. Do not let the false delights of a deceptive world deceive you. St. Clare of Assisi

Our soul is so specially loved by him who is the highest that it goes far beyond the ability of any creature to realize it.... There is no creature made who can realize how much, how sweetly and how tenderly our maker loves us. And therefore we can, with his grace and his help, stand in Spirit, gazing with endless wonder at this lofty, unmeasurable love beyond human scope the Almighty God has for us of his goodness.

Blessed Julian of Norwich

Every little glimpse that can be gained of God exceeds every pain and every joy that man can conceive without it. **St. Catherine of Genoa**

I had a serious fault.... If I began to realize that a person liked me, and I took to him myself, I would grow so fond of him that my memory would feel compelled to revert to him and I would always be thinking of him, without intentionally giving any offence to God.... But when once I had seen the great beauty of the Lord [in a vision] I saw no one by comparison on whom my thoughts wished to dwell. **St. Teresa of Avila**

Learn to abide with attention in loving waiting upon God in the state of quiet.

Contemplation is nothing else but a secret, peaceful and loving infusion of God, which, if admitted, will set the soul on fire with the Spirit of love. **St. John of the Cross**

It is an old custom of the servants of God to have some little prayers ready and to be frequently darting them up to heaven during the day, lifting their minds to God out of the mire of this world. **St. Philip Neri**

It is true that the voice of God, having once fully penetrated the heart, becomes strong as the tempest and loud as the thunder, but before reaching the heart it is as weak as a light breath which scarcely agitates the air. It shrinks from noise, and is silent amid agitation.

St. Ignatius Loyola

I need nothing but God, and to lose myself in the heart of God. **St. Margaret Mary Alacoque**

Never read books you are not sure about... even supposing these bad books are very well written from a literary point of view. Let me ask you this: would you drink something you knew was poisoned just because it was offered to you in a golden cup? **St. John Bosco**

It is a great sorrow for a soul that wishes to live far from the pomps and vanities to return to the world, to put up with idle and insipid conversations instead of talking to God alone, to open one's eyes to see nothing but the earth instead of visions of heaven. **St. Gemma Galgani**

If I looked into a mirror, and did not see my face, I should have the sort of feeling which actually comes upon me, when I look into this living busy world, and see no reflection of its Creator.... Were it not for this voice, speaking so clearly in my conscience and my heart, I should be an atheist....

Venerable John Henry Cardinal Newman

Your mind... should be full of love of God, forgetful of yourself. It should be full of the contemplation and joy of My beatitude, of compassion and sorrow for My sufferings, and of joy at My joys.... It should be a mind full of love for your neighbor for My sake, for I love all men as a father loves his children. It should be full of longing for the spiritual and material goods of all men for My sake. It should be a mind free, tranquil, at peace.... Do not be disturbed by little things. Throw all little matters aside and try to live at a very high level, not from pride but from love. **Venerable Charles de Foucauld**

At the heart of this ocean of vanities and festivals, I felt within my soul a burning desire to learn how to pray. I inquired, I read, I kept myself as much as I could in God's presence. This was enough to begin seeing a great light shed on the nothingness of worldly things, on the vanity of existence, on the beauty of God.

Servant of God Concepción Cabrera de Armida

You persist in being worldly, superficial, scatterbrained... because you are a coward. What is it but cowardice not to want to face yourself? **Venerable José Escriva**

7

Death to Life Everlasting

WITH THE EMPHASIS on looking young and beautiful and on personal achievement and fulfillment in this life, most of us tend to avoid the reality of death. But all of the glamorous advertisements and proud achievements in this life can't begin to compare to the joys of life-everlasting union with the God of perfect beauty and majesty. The good things of this life are simply a dress rehearsal for the next, and death is the curtain call.

All the saints felt the pull of eternity and wanted to bring all those they knew into a similar longing for what really can fulfill. It is reported that St. Teresa of Avila sometimes used to watch the clock and remark that her only consolation for the tedium of life was to realize that with each passing moment she was closer to eternity. St. Augustine thought that the only real joy was the hope of eternity.

✠ ✠ ✠

Let us consider, beloved, how the Lord is continually revealing to us the resurrection that is to be. Of this He has constituted the Lord Jesus Christ the first fruits, by raising Him from the dead. **Pope St. Clement I**

The root of all good works is the hope of the resurrection; for the expectation of the reward [moves] the soul to good works. **St. Cyril of Jerusalem**

For it is for him to fear death who is not willing to go to Christ. **St. Cyprian**

To the good man to die is gain. The foolish fear death as the greatest of evils, the wise desire it as a rest after labors and the end of ills. **St. Ambrose**

Of what consequence is it what kind of death puts an end to life, since he who has died once is not forced to go through the same ordeal a second time.

The bodies of the saints will therefore rise again free from every defect, from every deformity, as well as from every corruption, encumbrance, or hindrance. In this respect their freedom of action will be as complete as their happiness. **St. Augustine**

Life is union and junction of mind [spirit], soul and body; death is the disruption of their union; God preserves it all even after this disruption. **St. Anthony the Great**

A gentle maiden [Mary], having lodged a God in her womb, asks as its price, peace for the world, salvation for those who are lost, and life for the dead.

St. Peter Chrysologus

On the death of her baby:

I give thanks to Almighty God that He has not considered me unworthy to be the mother of a child admitted into the celestial kingdom. Having quitted the world in the white robe of his innocence, he will rejoice in the presence of God through all eternity.

St. Clotilda

I can never lose one whom I have loved unto the end; one to whom my soul cleaves so firmly that it can never be separated does not go away but only goes before. Be mindful of me when you come to where I shall follow you. **St. Bernard**

The whole of this present world has become mean and wearisome, and on the other hand the world to come has become so unspeakably desirable and dear that I hold all these passing things as light as thistledown. I am tired of "living." **St. Herman of Reichenau**

Blessed be God for our sister, the death of the body.

St. Francis of Assisi

Jesus is said to have told Gertrude "my heaven would not be complete without you." **St. Gertrude the Great**

On her deathbed:

I thank Thee, dear Lord, for having permitted my body to become weak and infirm, so that I could the more freely return my soul to Thee. **Blessed Margaret Colonna**

My understanding was lifted up into heaven, where I saw our Lord like a lord in his own house who has called all his valued servants and friends to a solemn feast... and [Christ] filled [the house] with joy and mirth. He himself endlessly gladdened and solaced his valued friends... with the marvelous melody of endless love in his own fair, blessed face. This glorious countenance of the godhead completely fills all heaven with joy and bliss.... God showed three degrees of bliss that every soul that has willingly served God... shall have in heaven. The first is the gratitude... he shall receive from our Lord God... the second is that all the blessed creatures who are in heaven shall see the glorious thanking... the third... is that it shall last forever.

Blessed Julian of Norwich

The martyrs desired death, not to fly labor, but to attain their goal. And why do they not fear death, from which man naturally shrinks? Because they had vanquished the natural love of their own bodies by divine and supernatural love. **St. Catherine of Siena**

I find only one fault with you, death, that you are too niggardly with those who long for you, and too lavish with those who flee from you.

I do not believe it would be possible to find any joy comparable to that of a soul in purgatory, except the joy of the blessed in paradise—a joy which goes on increasing day by day as God more and more flows in upon the soul, which he does abundantly in proportion as every hindrance to his entrance is consumed away.

St. Catherine of Genoa

I saw myself dying with a desire to see God, and I knew not how to seek that life other than by dying.

Over my spirit flash and float in divine radiancy the bright and glorious visions of the world to which I go.

St. Teresa of Avila

Life is uncertain and, in fact, may be very brief. If we compare it with eternity, [we] will clearly realize that it cannot be but more than an instant.

A happy death of all the things of life is our principal concern. For if we attain that, it matters little if we lose all the rest. But if we do not attain that, nothing else will be of any value. **Blessed Junipero Serra**

About to be martyred:
Come, my sweetest Jesus, that I may now be inseparably united to thee in time and eternity: welcome ropes, hurdles, gibbets, knives and butchery, welcome for the love of Jesus, my saviour. **Blessed Henry Morse**

I have no further desire to live and only think of giving my life to God. **St. Lugartha Lee Yu-Hye (Korean martyr)**

... Of that hour in which the soul wavers between its future and its present home, mine is transported at even the probability [of death] for the bonds that hold it have scarcely strength to restrain it... and if reason and the best affections of this world did not withhold and draw back with more than common force its flying propensities, I should have renounced every other desire and aim long ago. **St. Elizabeth Seton**

Eternity, eternity, when shall I come to You at last?... in eternity where we will love with a glance of the soul.

St. Elizabeth Seton

I shall be beheaded. Within a few short hours my soul will quit this earth, exile over, and battle won. I shall mount upwards and enter into our true home. There among God's elect I shall gaze upon what eye of man cannot imagine, hear undreamed of harmonies, enjoy a happiness the heart cannot comprehend.

St. Theophane Venard

On his deathbed:
What a beautiful thing I see. **St. Dominic Savio**

On his way to martyrdom:
Why should you bind me? From whom should I escape? From God? **St. Joseph Mukasa Balikuddembe**

I am not afraid. I have been waiting for my Lord for a long time. He is the one who has made me love death and now my one desire is to go and be with Him.

Blessed Rafka al-Rayes

Jesus, destroy this chain of a body, for I shall never be content till my soul can fly to you. When shall I be completely blessed in you? **St. Gemma Galgani**

Remember that you ought to die as a martyr, stripped of everything, stretched naked on the ground, unrecognizable, covered with wounds and blood, killed violently and painfully—and desire that it be today.... Think often of death, so as to prepare for it and appraise things at their true value.

Venerable Charles de Foucauld

There are difficulties, sufferings, and worries.... But one beautiful day it will be all over, and we will find ourselves all united in Heaven with the Blessed Trinity, with Mary most holy, with our dear ones and with the Sisters who have gone before us. This is our joy and our comfort. Courage! **Venerable Thecla Merlo**

You, if you are an apostle, will not have to die. You will move to a new house: that is all. **Venerable José Escriva**

8

Delusion to
Truth

OUR TIMES HAVE WITNESSED bewildering confusion about truth, especially about religious absolutes, even among Christians. First, many are so inundated with the general skepticism and relativism that marks modernity that they doubt if we can know anything at all with certainty. Others imagine that the only source of truth about eternal matters comes from personal experience. New Age philosophies play on the substitution of subjective intuition for solid doctrine.

Naturally, such states of intellectual confusion lead not only to inconsistent doctrinal pluralism but also to delusions about moral obligation. If we cannot know anything for certain, why follow any set of ethical teachings faithfully? Some suppose that even Scripture should be interpreted only personally, not authoritatively. Further, traditional religious authority is outmoded. Therefore, one is free to pick and choose from Scripture and Tradition since nothing is binding.

How different were the views of the saints! Eager to avoid the itching ears St. Paul warns of, holy Christians have clung to objective truth as revealed by God. Many of the Fathers of the Church, such as Saints Clement, Ambrose, and Augustine, spent years of intellectual toil defeating false teaching. Prophetic saints such as Dominic and Francis gave the lie to delusions of lax clergy and laity that piling up wealth or indulging in loose sexuality was permissible.

✠ ✠ ✠

He (Jesus) said that we must be slain and hated for His name's sake and that many prophets and false Christs would come forward in His name and would lead many astray. And this is the case. For many have taught what is godless and wicked, falsely stamping their teaching with His name and have taught what has been put into their mind by the unclean spirit of the devil.

St. Justin Martyr

Poor human reason when it trusts in itself substitutes the strangest absurdities for the highest divine concepts. **St. John Chrysostom**

Truly barren is profane education which is always in labor but never gives birth. For what fruit worthy of such pangs does philosophy show for being so long in labor? Do not all who are full of wind and never come to term miscarry before they come into the light of the knowledge of God? They could as well become men if they were not altogether hidden in the womb of barren wisdom. **Gregory of Nyssa**

That is true which is. Nothing is greater than the mind of man, except God. Learn to fix the eye of faith on the divine word of the Holy Scriptures as on a light shining in a dark place until the day dawn and the day-star arise in our hearts. For the ineffable source from which this lamp borrows its light is the Light that shines in darkness but the darkness does not comprehend it. To see it, our hearts must be purified by faith. **St. Augustine**

Since he is the Sun of Justice, he fittingly calls his disciples the light of the world. The reason for this is that through them, as through shining rays, he has poured out the light of the knowledge of himself upon the entire world. For by manifesting the light of truth, they have dispelled the darkness of error from the hearts of men. **St. Chromatius of Aquileia**

Lord, shed upon our darkened souls the brilliant light of your wisdom so that we may be enlightened and serve you with renewed purity. Sunrise marks the hour for men to begin their toil, but in our souls, Lord, prepare a dwelling for the day that will never end. Through our unremitting zeal for you, Lord, set upon us the sign of your day that is not measured by the sun.
St. Ephraem

Just as God's creature, the sun, is one and the same the world over, so also does the Church's preaching shine everywhere to enlighten all men who want to come to the knowledge of truth. **St. Irenaeus**

Teaching unsupported by grace may enter our ears, but it never reaches the heart. When God's grace does touch our innermost minds to bring understanding, then his word, which is received by the ear, can sink deep into the heart. **St. Isidore of Seville**

Most high, glorious God, enlighten the darkness of my heart and give me, Lord, a correct faith, a certain hope, a perfect charity, sense, and knowledge, so that I may carry out your holy and true command. **St. Francis of Assisi**

So long as we are still in this place of pilgrimage, so long as men's hearts are crooked and prone to sin, lazy and feeble in virtue, we need to be encouraged and roused, so that brother may be helped by brother and the eagerness of heavenly love rekindle the flame in our spirit which our everyday carelessness and tepidity tend to extinguish. **Blessed Jordan of Saxony**

In Him, therefore, do I understand and possess all truth that is in heaven and earth and hell, and in all creatures; and so great is the truth and the certainty that were the whole world to declare the contrary I would not believe it, yea, I should mock at it.

Blessed Angela of Foligno

Happy the man whose words issue from the Holy Spirit and not from himself. **St. Anthony of Padua**

You are a fire that takes away the coldness, illuminates the mind with its light, and causes me to know your truth. **St. Catherine of Siena**

When St. Paul's voice was raised to preach the gospel to all nations, it was like a great clap of thunder in the sky. His preaching was a blazing fire carrying all before it. It was the sun rising in full glory. Infidelity was consumed by it, false beliefs fled away, and the truth appeared like a great candle lighting the whole world with its brilliant flame. **St. Bernardino of Siena**

All who undertake to teach must be endowed with deep love, the greatest patience, and, most of all, profound humility. They must perform their work with earnest zeal. Then through their humble prayers, the Lord will find them worthy to become fellow workers with him in the cause of truth. **St. Joseph of Calasanza**

Who is there in this illustrious home of learning who does not think daily as he goes to the schools of law, medicine, philosophy, or theology, how best he may progress in his particular subject and at last win his doctor's degree? Well, the school of Christ is the school of charity. In the last day,... charity will be the whole syllabus. **St. Robert Bellarmine**

Reason and human science often lead you into error because they are too weak and limited to penetrate to the knowledge of the things of God, which are infinite and incomprehensible. Human intelligence and knowledge also deceive you, because they are too full of darkness and obscurity of sin to attain to a genuine knowledge even of things outside of God. **St. John Eudes**

When I see the need there is for divine teaching and how hungry people are to hear it, I am atremble to be off and running throughout the world, preaching the word of God. I have no rest, my soul finds no other relief than to rush about and preach. **St. Anthony Mary Claret**

Those who are led by the Holy Spirit have true ideas; that is why so many ignorant people are wiser than the learned. The Holy Spirit is light and strength.

St. John Vianney

Truth is one; therefore... the multitude of men are wrong, as far as they differ; and as they differ, not about trivial points, but about great matters, it follows that the multitude of men, whether by their own fault or not, are wrong even in the greater matters of religion.... Truth addressed itself to our spiritual nature; it will be greatly understood, valued by none but lovers of truth, virtue, purity, humility, and peace.

Venerable John Henry Cardinal Newman

9

Despair to Hope

IN OUR MODERN SOCIETY, which tends to devalue and even reject solid Christian values, there is a decided absence of hope and a tendency toward despair. Suicide is the final act in the tragedy of despair that can conquer even such brilliant individuals as Vincent Van Gogh and Ernest Hemingway, to mention just two. Indeed, it is hard to imagine why suicide would not seem to be the way out of pain and disillusionment without strong hope in God and everlasting life as the reward for maintaining hope and trust in this life.

Scripture teaches us that "with God all things are possible" (Mt 19:26). Consider the contrast between the apostles Peter and Judas. St. Peter denied the Lord and Judas betrayed him. Both had seriously damaged their relationship with the Lord and could have lost hope, but St. Peter trusted in the mercy of Jesus, believing that even forgiveness for denying his Lord was possible to God. But Judas gave in to despair and hanged himself.

In more recent times, Venerable Francis Libermann tells that he could not pass a bridge without wanting to jump off. He prayed and God gave him grace to hope instead of despair.

☒ ☒ ☒

No one is safe by his own strength, but he is safe by the grace and mercy of God. **St. Cyprian**

We need not despair of any man, so long as he lives.
For God deemed it better to bring good out of evil than not to permit evil at all. **St. Augustine**

Hope always draws the soul from the beauty that is seen to what is beyond, always kindles the desire for the hidden through what is perceived. **St. Gregory of Nyssa**

If Christ is with us, who is against us? You can fight with confidence where you are sure of victory. With Christ and for Christ victory is certain. **St. Bernard**

I am concealing Myself [Christ] from you so that you can discover by yourself what you are without Me.

St. Margaret of Cortona

Christ did give the devil power over Him that He might be tempted and led into danger and persecuted even unto death, in order that He might thereby liberate man from the devil's power.
When I was in the darkness of spirit methought I would have chosen rather to be roasted than to endure such pains. Wherefore did I cry aloud and call upon

death, desiring that it should come in any form whatsoever if only God would permit me to die.

Blessed Angela of Foligno

Perfection does not consist in consolation, but rather in the submission of our wills to God, above all in desolation. Let us remember that the obedience of our Lord was perfect when his mouth and tongue burned with the fever of his wounds, and this was only increased and his thirst became greater when they gave him gall and vinegar to drink. **Blessed Henry Suso**

We [should] seek him determinedly and diligently without sloth, as well as we can, through his grace, and we should do so gladly and merrily, without unreasonable depression and vain sorrow.

It belongs to the proper goodness of our Lord God courteously to excuse man. **Blessed Julian of Norwich**

The time will come when there shall be one flock and one shepherd, one faith and one clear knowledge of God. **St. Birgitta of Sweden**

The most hopeful people in the world are the young and the drunk. The first because they have little experience of failure, and the second because they have succeeded in drowning theirs. **St. Thomas Aquinas**

Let the world indulge its madness, for it cannot endure and passes like a shadow. It is growing old, and I think, is in its last decrepit stage. But we, buried deep in the wounds of Christ, why should we be dismayed?

St. Peter Canisius

*When the cart she was riding in overturned during a journey
to found a Carmelite convent, St. Teresa was heard to pray to
God:*
No wonder you have so few friends, since this is the way
you treat them. **St. Teresa of Avila**

If we are to rise above this depression, dejection, and
despondency of soul and turn it to use in God's service,
we must face it, accept it, and realize the worth of holy
self-abasement. In this way you will transmute the lead
of your heaviness into gold, a gold far purer than any of
your gayest, most light-hearted sallies.

The past must be abandoned to God's mercy, the
present to our fidelity, the future to divine providence.

St. Francis de Sales

Cast yourself into the arms of God and be very sure
that if He wants anything of you, He will fit you for the
work and give you strength. **St. Philip Neri**

Conceal yourself in Jesus crucified, and hope for nothing except that all men be thoroughly converted to his
will. **St. Paul of the Cross**

God is so good and merciful, that to obtain Heaven it is
sufficient to ask it of Him from our hearts.

St. Benedict Joseph Labré

I ought to have a heart burning with love, but I am only
a reservoir of frozen water.... A soul in purgatory lives
without light because it cannot see God, without joy
because it cannot possess him; but it is fully and always
obedient to him. **Blessed Eugénie Smet**

When tempted to despair, I have only one resource: to throw myself at the foot of the tabernacle like a little dog at the foot of his master. **St. John Vianney**

If I saw the gates of Hell open and I stood on the brink of the abyss, I should not despair, I should not lose hope of mercy, because I should trust in Thee, my God.

St. Gemma Galgani

However wicked I may be, however great a sinner, I *must* hope that I should go to heaven. You forbid me to despair. **Venerable Charles de Foucauld**

... Suddenly, when the soul is engulfed in pain, at these very moments, almost of despair, there comes a gentle breeze, changing parching arid suffering into a pleasant freshness without other desire than to please the Beloved, without dreaming any more about the pleasure of future goods.

Servant of God Concepción Cabrera de Armida

The most beautiful Credo is the one we pronounce in our hour of darkness. **Servant of God Padre Pio**

Anyone else would be a saint by now, you told me and I... I'm always the same! Son, I replied, keep up your daily communion, and think: what would I be if I had not gone? **Venerable José Escriva**

10

Disorder to Self-Control

THE FOCUS TODAY UPON ADDICTIVE BEHAVIORS reminds us how disordered many of our lives have become whether it be addiction to alcohol or drugs, or a compulsion to overeat. By contrast the saints exemplify self-control, a fruit of the Holy Spirit (Gal 5:23).

When I think of self-control, the first saint that comes to mind is St. Thérèse of Lisieux, whose little way of love took the Catholic world by storm. She was convinced that for herself, and for most Christians, it is not large courageous feats that God wants but doing each little thing out of love. That meant heroic self-control over impulses to anger or dislike. So adept did she become at her own little way that people she felt an aversion for would imagine they gave her special joy. Another example is St. Catherine of Siena. Though she was a virgin who was never known to commit a single sin of impurity, she was nonetheless plagued by interior temptations to such sins. God's grace of self-control saved her from any exterior sign of this struggle.

✠ ✠ ✠

We should not engage in fruitless or controversial discussions. **St. Basil**

Drunkenness is the ruin of reason. It is premature old age. It is temporary death. **St. Basil**

Those whose hearts are pure are the temples of the Holy Spirit. **St. Lucy**

He who is educated and eloquent must not measure his saintliness merely by his fluency. Of two imperfect things, holy rusticity is better than sinful eloquence.

St. Jerome

Do not say that you have chaste minds if you have unchaste eyes, because an unchaste eye is the messenger of an unchaste heart.

Lust served became a custom, and custom not resisted became necessity.

The devil invented gambling. **St. Augustine**

Those whose will always inclines to self-indulgence refuse to do even what is in their power under the pretext that they have no help from above. **St. Mark the Ascetic**

Truly my soul is troubled and my spirit freezes at the fact that, although we are given freedom to choose and do the deeds of the saints, we are intoxicated by passions, as though drunk with wine, and do not want to lift our minds on high and seek higher glory, do not want to imitate the deeds of the saints nor follow in their footsteps, to become heirs of their works and receive with them an eternal heritage.

He alone is intelligent who tries to please God and is mostly silent, or, if he speaks, speaks little—and says only what is necessary and pleasing to God.

St. Anthony the Great

The drunken man is a living corpse.... Wine is given us of God, not that we might be drunken, but that we might be sober; that we might be glad, not that we get ourselves pain. St. John Chrysostom

To keep one's mouth from evil and depraved talk; not to love much speaking. St. Benedict

Nothing is sweeter than the calm of conscience: nothing safer than purity of soul, which yet no one can bestow on itself because it is properly the gift of another.

St. Columbanus

Silence of the lips is better and more wonderful than any edifying conversation.... But since, in our weakness, we cannot yet follow the path of the perfect, let us talk of what edifies. St. Barsanuphius

There is one sort of temperance for those of good conduct and another for those inclined to particular weaknesses. Among the former any kind of bodily stirring evokes an immediate urge to restraint, while among the latter there is no relief or relaxation from such stirrings until the very day they die. The former strive always for peace of mind, while the latter try to appease God by their contrition.

Gluttony is hypocrisy of the stomach. Filled, it moans about scarcity; stuffed and crammed, it wails about hunger. **St. John Climacus**

Inordinate love of the flesh is cruelty, because under the appearance of pleasing the body we kill the soul.

Take even bread with moderation, lest an overloaded stomach make you weary of prayer. **St. Bernard**

A man who governs his passions is master of the world. We must either command them, or be enslaved by them. It is better to be a hammer than an anvil.

St. Dominic

Do you not know that fasting can master concupiscence, lift up the soul, confirm it in the paths of virtue, and prepare a fine reward for the Christian?

St. Hedwig of Silesia

Irrational feeding darkens the soul and makes it unfit for spiritual experiences. **St. Thomas Aquinas**

When it seems that God shows us the faults of others, keep on the safer side—it may be that thy judgement is false. On thy lips let silence abide.... If the vice really exists in a person, he will correct himself better, seeing himself so gently understood, and will say of his own accord the things thou wouldst have said to him.

St. Catherine of Siena

Our self-will is so subtle and so deeply-rooted within us, so covered with excuses and defended by false reasoning that it seems a devil. When we cannot do our own will in any way, we do it in another, under all kinds of pretexts—of charity, of necessity, of justice... from the example of others, or of pleasing someone who is trying to oblige us. St. Catherine of Genoa

None who are wise in words have ever had pure reason, because... they let their reasoning powers be corrupted by unseemly thoughts. St. Gregory of Sinai

Disorder in society is the result of disorder in the family. St. Angela Merici

I am trying as hard as ever I can to keep my splendor and dignity [as a Cardinal] as modest as can be. Indeed within the limits of decorum and dignity, I am just not shabby. St. Robert Bellarmine

Be not curious about matters that do not concern thee; never speak of them, and do not ask about them.

St. Teresa of Avila

Frequent not the company of immodest persons, especially if they are also imprudent, as is generally the case.

He who could take away detraction from the world, would take away from it a great part of its sins and iniquities. St. Francis de Sales

Never utter in your neighbour's absence what you would not say in their presence. St. Mary Magdalene dei Pazzi

As long as a single passion reigns in our hearts, though all the others should have been overcome, the soul will never enjoy peace. St. Joseph Calasanctius

It is almost certain that excess in eating is the cause of almost all the diseases of the body, but its effects on the soul are even more disastrous.

We must mortify our tongue, by abstaining from words of detraction, abuse, and obscenity. An impure word spoken in jest may prove a scandal to others, and sometimes a word of double meaning, said in a witty way, does more harm than a word openly impure.

St. Alphonsus Liguori

What will [the vain woman] not do and suffer to preserve the beauty necessary for her ends.... What torment will she not inflict on body, head and hair before her vanity is satisfied.... She must act a hundred parts... and at the end of the day things did not go as one hoped. Someone else drew all eyes and attention. Nothing is brought home but disappointment and bitterness. **Blessed Claude de la Colombierè**

Nothing can be more dangerous than evil companions. They communicate the infection of their vices to all who associate with them.

Would we wish that our own hidden sins should be divulged? We ought, then, to be silent regarding those of others. **St. John Baptiste de la Salle**

Holy purity, the queen of virtues, the angelic virtue, is a jewel so precious that those who possess it become like the angels of God in heaven, even though clothed in mortal flesh.

Avoid those who in your presence are not ashamed to make use of scandalous words, and expressions of double meaning. **St. John Bosco**

Speak little to creatures but speak much with God. He will make you truly wise. **St. Mary Mazzarello**

Silence is a gift of God, to let us speak more intimately with God. **St. Vincent Pallotti**

By force of events, you made me chaste.... Chastity became a blessing and inner necessity to me. It was you who did that, O God—you alone. I, alas, had no part in it. How good you have been! From what sad and culpable relapses you miraculously preserved me!... The devil is too much the master of an unchaste soul to let truth enter it. You could not, O God, come into a soul where the devil of unbridled passions rules supreme. But you wanted to come into my soul, O good shepherd, and you yourself expelled your enemy from it.

Venerable Charles de Foucauld

Here was one lady talking about my pretty hair and another, just going out the door wanting to know who that very pretty girl was.... The thrill of pleasure I felt made me realize that I was full of self-love. I am always ready to sympathize with the people who lose their souls—after all, it's so easy, once you begin to stray along the primrose path of worldliness.

St. Thérèse of Lisieux

Never rise from the table, moreover, without having given due thanks to the Lord. If we act in this way we need have no fear of the wretched sin of gluttony. As you eat, take care not to be too difficult to please in the matter of food, bearing in mind that it is very easy to give in to gluttony. Never eat more than you really need.... I don't mean to say that you should rise from table without eating. No, this is not my intention. Let everything be regulated by prudence which should be the rule in all our actions. **Servant of God Padre Pio**

Purity? They ask. And they smile. They are the very people who approach marriage with worn-out bodies and disillusioned minds.

How I wish your bearing and conversation were such that, on seeing or hearing you, people would say: this man reads the life of Jesus Christ. **Venerable José Escriva**

11

Distance to
Intimacy with God

HOW MANY OF US MAINTAIN A certain distance in our relationships because we are afraid of the demands
of a more intimate tie? This is a pity because we also
lose the joy of shared life. With God such distancing
makes no sense since we were made to know, love, and
serve him.

How sad that God may be drawing us closer and
closer to him, but we prefer to remain distant, safe on
our own territory, and seemingly in control. The saints
lure us into praying for greater intimacy with the God
of love.

St. Catherine of Genoa is a fascinating example of a
woman who tried to avoid intimacy with God by plung-
ing into social life, only to finally remove herself from
all but the society of other holy people and those with
repulsive diseases. She learned the importance of an
intimate relationship with God. In fact, for all the saints
who knew God intimately in childhood, there are many
others who led a worldly life up to a certain point.
Venerable Charles de Foucauld is a fine example. He

led the life of a worldly and sinful soldier only to end up living the life of a hermit in the desert!

✠ ✠ ✠

Christ made my soul beautiful with the jewels of grace and virtue. I belong to Him whom the angels serve.

St. Agnes

Only one thing is impossible for man—to avoid death. To have communion with God is possible for him, if he understands how it is possible. For if he wishes and understands [how it is to be done] through faith and love, testified by a good life, a man can commune with God. **St. Anthony the Great**

Too late have I loved Thee, O Beauty of ancient days, yet ever new! Too late have I loved Thee! And lo! Thou wert within, and I abroad searching for Thee. Thou wert with me, but I was not with Thee.

This is our daily bread [Holy Communion]; take it daily, that it may profit thee daily. Live, as to deserve to receive it daily. **St. Augustine**

Invisible in His own nature [God] became visible in ours. Beyond our grasp, He chose to come within our grasp. **St. Leo the Great**

For the soul is the inner face of man, by which we are known, that we may be regarded with love by our maker. **St. Gregory the Great**

Poor creature though I be, I am the hand and foot of Christ. I move my hand and my hand is wholly Christ's hand, for deity is become inseparably one with me. I move my good and it is aglow with God.

St. Simeon the New Theologian

Let us learn to cast our hearts into God. **St. Bernard**

His divinity is never foreign to me. For always and without any fetters I feel it in every one of my limbs.... The soul ran out originally from God's heart and must needs return there. **St. Mechtild of Magdeburg**

So, abandon yourself utterly for the love of God, and in this way you will become truly happy. **Blessed Henry Suso**

God loves all existing things.
     To love God is something greater than to know Him.
     The end of my labors has come. All that I have written appears to me as much straw after the things that have been revealed to me. **St. Thomas Aquinas**

In beautiful things St. Francis saw Beauty itself, and through His vestiges imprinted on creation he followed his Beloved everywhere, making from all things a ladder by which he could climb up and embrace Him who is utterly desirable.
     If you desire to know... ask grace, not instruction; desire, not understanding; the groaning of prayer, not diligent reading; the Spouse, not the teacher; God, not man; darkness not clarity; not light, but the fire that totally inflames and carries us into God by ecstatic unctions and burning affections. **St. Bonaventure**

I saw that for us He is everything that is good, comforting and helpful; He is our clothing, who, for love, wraps us up, holds us close; He entirely encloses us for tender love, so that He may never leave us, since He is the source of all good things for us, as I understood it.

Blessed Julian of Norwich

Those in the state of union with God on earth are en- flamed and submerged in the blood, where they find my [God's] burning charity. This charity is a fire that comes forth from me and carries off their heart and spirit, accepting the sacrifice of their desires. Then their mind's eye rises up and gazes into my Godhead, and love follows understanding to be nourished there and brought into the union....

You [God] are a fire that takes away the coldness, illuminates the mind with its light, and causes me to know your truth and I know that you are beauty and wisdom itself. The food of angels, you give yourself to man in the fire of your love.

For perfected souls every place is to them an oratory.

St. Catherine of Siena

I am no longer my own. Whether I live or whether I die, I belong to my Saviour. I have nothing of my own. God is my all, and my whole being is His.

I will have nothing to do with a love that would be *for* God or *in* God. I cannot bear the words *for* or the word *in*, because they denote something that may be in between God and me. **St. Catherine of Genoa**

The soul that is united with God is feared by the devil as one who is where God Himself is. **St. John of the Cross**

Make many acts of love, for they set the soul on fire and make it gentle.

Whatever thou doest, offer it up to God, and pray it may be for His honor and glory. **St. Teresa of Avila**

In the royal galley of Divine Love, there are no galley slaves: all the rowers are volunteers.

The end of love is no other than the union of the lover and the thing loved. **St. Francis de Sales**

A Christian has a union with Jesus Christ more noble, more intimate and more perfect than the members of a human body have with their head.

He longs to be in you, he wants his breath to be your breath, his heart in your heart, and his soul in your soul. **St. John Eudes**

I have no doubt that this divine Saviour possesses you since you wish to be hidden in him. It is why I look for you there, I find you there, I see you there, there I love and cherish you.

To be separated from Jesus Christ is to have no faith; or if one does have it, not to live by his spirit or his grace so as to become dead, withered members, still attached to the body but as if they were not because they do not participate in the spiritual life which animates the body. **Blessed Marie of the Incarnation**

Nothing but self-will can separate us from God.

There are certain souls who desire to arrive at perfection all at once, and this desire keeps them in constant disquiet. It is necessary first to cling to the feet of Jesus, then to kiss his sacred hands, and at last you may find your way into his divine heart.

Love tends to union with the object loved. Now Jesus

Christ loves a soul that is in a state of grace with an immense love; He ardently desires to unite Himself with it. This is what Holy Communion does.

St. Alphonsus Liguori

The Lord pursued me for a long time... but invariably I again attached myself to nothingness in order to shun the abyss of love Jesus had in store for me.

St. Peter Julian Eymard

My sovereign Master showed me that my soul was the blank canvas on which He wished to paint all the details of His life of suffering, entirely spent in love and poverty, solitude, silence and sacrifice till the end.

The heart of Jesus desires to be everything to the heart that it loves. But that will only be by suffering for Him. **St. Margaret Mary Alacoque**

Regarding the Eucharist:
How sweet, the presence of Jesus to the longing, harassed soul! It is instant peace, and balm to every wound. **St. Elizabeth Seton**

When I am before the Blessed Sacrament I feel such a lively faith that I cannot describe it. Christ in the Eucharist is almost tangible to me. To kiss his wounds continually and embrace him. When it is time for me to leave I have to tear myself away from his sacred presence. **St. Anthony Mary Claret**

When entering and leaving my room and on other occasions when I am able, having first cast myself down on my knees I will imagine that the Lord comes down to me with the abundance of his grace; I also believe that he will communicate Himself to me and become one with me totally. St. Vincent Pallotti

Holy Communion is the shortest and safest way to heaven. There are others: innocence, but that is for little children; penance, but we are afraid of it; generous endurance of trials of life, but when they come we weep and ask to be spared. The surest, easiest, shortest way is the Eucharist. St. Pius X

To decorate the houses with religious pictures is a custom as old as Christianity itself, for the true Christian has always considered his home as nothing less than a Temple of God, and the religious pictures as means to extend and preserve the spirit of Christianity in the home.

Our home is—Heaven. On earth we are like travelers staying at a hotel. When one is away, one is always thinking of home.

[Mary] seeks for those who approach her devoutly and with reverence, for such she loves, nourishes, and adopts as her children.

Upon receiving Holy Communion, the Adorable Blood of Jesus Christ really flows in our veins and His flesh is really blended with ours.... When Our Lord sees pure souls coming eagerly to visit him in the Blessed Sacrament he smiles on them. They come with the simplicity that pleases him so much.

The interior life is like a sea of love in which the soul is plunged and is, as it were, drowned in love. Just as a mother holds her child's face in her hands to cover it with kisses, so does God hold the devout man.

St. John Vianney

Oh, if all were to know how beautiful Jesus is, how amiable He is! They would all die of love. **St. Gemma Galgani**

Our Lord does not come down from Heaven every day to lie in a golden ciborium. He comes to find another heaven which is infinitely dearer to Him—the heaven of our souls. **St. Thérèse of Lisieux**

He loves, He hopes, He waits. If He came down on our altars on certain days only, some sinner, on being moved to repentance, might have to look for Him, and not finding Him have to wait. Our Lord prefers to wait Himself for the sinner for years rather than keep him waiting an instant.

The Holy Eucharist is the perfect expression of the love of Jesus Christ for man, since it is the quintessence of all the mysteries of His life.

I can no longer live without Jesus. How soon shall I receive Him again? **St. Maria Goretti**

When I was around fifteen or sixteen, I was permitted to receive [Holy Communion] four or five times a week, and, soon after, every day. I was happy, so happy when I could receive! It is an absolute necessity of my life. **Servant of God Concepción Cabrera de Armida**

If you ate only one meal a week would you survive? It is the same for your soul. Nourish it with the Blessed Sacrament. A nice dish is set there for us, with something good on it—we don't pay any attention to it.

Blessed Brother André

In this sad world, there is a joy at the heart of things which is not shared by either the saints in heaven or the angels—that of suffering with our beloved. However hard life may be, however long our days of sadness may endure... we must never seek to leave the foot of the cross sooner than God would have us do... our master having been good enough to let us experience, if not always its sweetness, then at least its beauty and necessity for those who love it. **Venerable Charles de Foucauld**

God wants to wed the soul in faith and the soul which is to celebrate this heavenly marriage must walk in pure faith, which is the only suitable means for this loving union. **Servant of God Padre Pio**

Anything that does not lead you to God is a hindrance. Root it out and throw it far from you. **Venerable José Escriva**

12

Doubt to Faith

IN CHAPTER EIGHT, we heard from the saints about the need to move from delusion to truth. Now the saints will help us journey from doubt to faith. In our skeptical times some teachers give the impression that doubt is not only a negative but a positive state of realizing that there is no absolute truth. This is simply false.

Since "faith is the hope of things unseen" (Heb 11:1), it is vital that we find ways to overcome doubt and renew faith in God, ourselves, and others, through the grace of the Holy Spirit. Naturally, the human mind, wounded by sin, will often find reasons to doubt another or to question a teaching of the faith. But we need to move beyond doubt, through prayer and study, to understand how great a gift it is to cling to God in faith even when all is not clear. Once gifted with faith, we must try to understand what we believe so that we can better teach it to others.

An interesting example of journeying from doubt to faith can be found in the life of St. Jeanne de Chantal. The daughter of a lawyer, Jeanne was well-educated.

She lived in a time in France when many had come to doubt their Catholic faith and had turned instead to Calvinistic beliefs. Although after her widowhood she was eager to serve the church as a disciple and co-foundress of the Visitation Order with St. Francis de Sales, she had bouts of interior darkness where the truths of the faith ceased to radiate with light. Instead of making a public show of her doubts, Jeanne confided them trustingly to her saintly spiritual director. St. Francis advised her never to take action based on doubt and confusion, but to honor God by giving herself to the works she had undertaken in a time of light with the same fervor. Eventually, she was given the gift of peace of mind concerning doctrinal questions.

✠ ✠ ✠

Just as God's creature, the sun, is one and the same the world over, so also does the Church's preaching shine everywhere to enlighten all men who want to come to a knowledge of the truth. **St. Irenaeus**

A man who is well grounded in the testimonies of the Scripture is the bulwark of the Church. **St. Jerome**

It is faith which delivers through the blood of Christ.

St. Ambrose

Just as at the sea those who are carried away from the direction of the harbor bring themselves back on course by a clear sign, so Scripture may guide those adrift on the sea of life back into the harbor of the divine will. **St. Gregory of Nyssa**

Poor human reason when it trusts in itself substitutes the strangest absurdities for the highest divine concepts. St. John Chrysostom

God is not a deceiver, that he should offer to support us, and then, when we lean upon Him, should slip away from us. St. Augustine

People are generally called intelligent through a wrong use of this word. The intelligent are not those who have studied the sayings and writings of the wise men of old, but those whose soul is intelligent, who can judge what is good and what evil; they avoid what is evil and harms the soul and intelligently care for and practice what is good and profits the world, greatly thanking God. St. Anthony the Great

God is the beginning, the middle and the end of every good. But the good cannot become active or be believed in otherwise than in Jesus Christ and the Holy Spirit. St. Mark the Ascetic

The Lord opened the understanding of my unbelief that, even though late... I might turn with all my heart to the Lord my God, who regarded my low estate, and pitied the youth of my ignorance, and kept me before I knew him, and before I had discernment. St. Patrick

If a man is firm in faith he will never be confused in discussions and disputes with heretics or unbelievers, because he has in him Jesus, the Lord of peace and quiet. After a peaceful discussion, such a man can lovingly bring many heretics and unbelievers to the knowledge of Jesus Christ Our Saviour. St. Barsanuphius

The disbelief of Thomas has done more for our faith than the faith of the other disciples. As he touches Christ and is won over to belief, every doubt is cast aside and our faith is strengthened. St. Gregory the Great

The Church is like a great ship being pounded by the waves of life's different stresses. Our duty is not to abandon ship, but to keep her on her course. St. Boniface

Faith is readiness to die for Christ's sake, for His commandments, in the conviction that such death brings life; it is to regard poverty as riches, insignificance and nothingness as true fame and glory and, having nothing, to be sure you possess all things. But above all, faith is attainment of [the] invisible treasure of the knowledge of Christ. St. Simeon the New Theologian

Who teaches the soul, if not God? There is no better instruction for the world than that which comes from God. St. Clare of Montefalco

Faith seeks understanding.
    I do not seek to understand that I may believe, but I believe in order to understand. St. Anselm

Although our view of the sublimist things is limited and weak, it is most pleasant to be able to catch but a glimpse of them.
    Three things are necessary for the salvation of man:

to know what he ought to believe; to know what he ought to desire; and to know what he ought to do.

Even some things which reason is able to investigate must be held by faith; so that all may share in the knowledge of God easily, and without doubt and error.

St. Thomas Aquinas

The Trinity is our maker. The Trinity is our keeper. The Trinity is our everlasting lover. The Trinity is our endless joy. **Blessed Julian of Norwich**

Holy Spirit, Spirit of truth, you are the reward of the saints, the comforter of souls, light in the darkness, riches to the poor, treasure to lovers, food for the hungry, comfort to those who are wandering; to sum up, you are the one in whom all treasures are contained.

St. Mary Magdalene dei Pazzi

I am a daughter of the Church. **St. Teresa of Avila**

It is because of faith that we exchange the present for the future.

What made the holy apostles and martyrs endure fierce agony and bitter torments, except faith, and especially faith in the resurrection? **St. Fidelis of Sigmaringen**

Without faith no one can please God, and without pleasing God no one can be saved, and seeing there is no faith save that which Christ taught to his apostles, it behoveth every man to find the faith and to live and die in it, even though they lose the world thereby, for it means life and death forever. **Venerable William Lloyd**

Faith is a divine and celestial light, a participation in the eternal, inaccessible light, a beam radiating from the face of God. St. John Eudes

We should submit our reason to the truths of faith with the humility and simplicity of a child. St. Alphonsus Liguori

The eyes of the world see no further than this life, as mine see no further than this wall when the church door is shut. The eyes of the Christian see deep into eternity. St. John Vianney

Do things simply, without too much analysis.

Venerable Francis Libermann

From the age of fifteen, dogma has been the fundamental principle of my religion: I know of no other religion, I cannot enter into the idea of any other sort of religion; religion, as a mere sentiment, is to me a dream and a mockery.

A thousand difficulties do not make a single doubt.

Venerable John Henry Cardinal Newman

Oh how glorious our Faith is! Instead of restricting hearts, as the world fancies, it uplifts them and enlarges their capacity to love. St. Thérèse of Lisieux

The moment I realized that God existed, I knew that I could not do otherwise than to live for Him alone.... Faith strips the mask from the world and reveals God in everything. It makes nothing impossible and renders meaningless such words as anxiety, danger, and fear, so that the believer goes through life calmly and peace-fully, with profound joy—like a child hand in hand with his mother. **Venerable Charles de Foucauld**

When you seek truth you seek God whether you know it or not. **Blessed Theresia Benedicta (Edith Stein)**

There are some who pass through life as through a tun-nel, without ever understanding the splendour and the security and the warmth of the sun of faith.

Venerable José Escriva

13

Emptiness to Fullness

HOW OFTEN WE COMPLAIN OF THE EMPTINESS and tedium of daily life! Yet the saints teach us to see in this void a sign that God has made us for something more than the world can give. After all, lower creatures are easily satisfied if they have food, warmth, sex, and sleep. But we have been created with what Pascal called "a God-sized vacuum" in our souls. And, at privileged moments, even on earth we get a foretaste of the fullness that awaits us when we will be united to God in eternity.

For example, St. Monica, who had suffered so long in her efforts to convert her son, St. Augustine, to the Catholic faith, enjoyed a beautiful time with him after his conversion just before her own death. Together they were looking out at the sea, and they seemed to have had a simultaneous mystical experience of the fullness of God's love. Blessed Mariam Baouardy, an Arab Carmelite of the nineteenth century, was so full of the Spirit that she would levitate into the air and perch on the limbs of trees singing songs of joy to the

Lord. These miracles were attested to by many eye-witnesses.

✠ ✠ ✠

With God nothing is empty of meaning, nothing without symbolism. St. Irenaeus

As a woman, compelled by natural affection, hastens to feed her babe from her overflowing breast, so also Christ ever nourishes with His blood those whom He regenerates. St. John Chrysostom

In the practice of virtues:
The fear of Gehenna encourages beginners to avoid evil disposition; and desire of good reward gives those who make progress, zeal to accomplish what is good. But the mystery of love exalts the mind above all created things, blinding it to all that is not God. For only those who have become blind to all that is below God, does the Lord give wisdom showing them the most Divine.

St. Mark the Ascetic

Restless are our hearts until they rest in Thee. All abundance which is not from God to me is neediness. This, then, is the full satisfaction of souls, this is the happy life: to recognize piously and completely the One through Whom you are led into the truth, the nature of the truth you enjoy, and the bond that connects you with the supreme measure. St. Augustine

There are in truth three states of the converted: the beginning, the middle, and the perfection. In the beginning they experience the charms of sweetness, in the middle the contests of temptation, and in the end the plenitude of perfection. **St. Gregory the Great**

I was made of love... therefore, in the nobility of my nature, no creature can suffice me and none open me, save Love alone. **St. Mechtild of Magdeburg**

From my infancy until now, in the seventieth year of my age, my soul has always beheld this sight.... The brightness which I see is not limited by space and is more brilliant than the radiance around the Sun.... Sometimes when I see it, all sadness and pain is lifted from me, and I seem a simple girl again, and an old woman no more.

St. Hildegarde

After Holy Communion:
This morning my soul is greater than the world since it possesses You, You whom heaven and earth do not contain. **St. Margaret of Cortona**

If any one of you be for a time cast down with weariness of spirit or afflicted with aridity of heart so that the torrent of devoted love seem to be dried up... realize the Lord's way. For a time He will draw away from you that you may seek Him with great ardor, and having sought may find Him with greater joy, and having found may hold Him with greater love, and having held may never let Him go. **Blessed Jordan of Saxony**

A true sanctuary, even before the future life, is a heart free from thoughts, made active by the Spirit. For there all is said and done spiritually. He who has not attained to such a state, although for the sake of some virtues he can be a stone suitable for us in building a temple to

God, is not himself a temple nor a celebrant of the Spirit. **St. Gregory of Sinai**

Grace has five effects in us: first, our soul is healed; second, we will good; third, we work effectively for it; fourth, we persevere; fifth, we break through to glory.

St. Thomas Aquinas

In God alone is there primordial and true delight, and in all our delights it is this delight that we are seeking.

St. Bonaventure

The reason we are not fully at ease in heart and soul is because we seek rest in these things that are so little and have no rest within them, and pay no attention to our God, who is Almighty, All-wise, All-good, and the only real rest. **Blessed Julian of Norwich**

In contemplation are great dishes of food and drink, of which no one knows save he who tastes them: but full satisfaction in fruition is the dish which is lacking there, and therefore this hunger is ever renewed. Yet, in the touch, rivers of honey, full of all delights, flow forth.

Blessed Jan Van Ruysbroeck

For it is of the nature of love, to love when it feels itself loved, and to love all things loved of its beloved. So when the soul has by degrees known the love of its Creator towards it, it loves Him, and, loving Him, loves all things whatsoever that God loves. **St. Catherine of Siena**

So abandon yourself utterly for the love of God, and in this way you will become truly happy. **Blessed Henry Suso**

Since I began to love, love has never forsaken me. It has ever grown to its own fullness within my innermost heart. **St. Catherine of Genoa**

If God has stripped you of the sense of His presence, it is in order that even His presence may no longer occupy your heart, but Himself. **St. Francis de Sales**

I saw everything beneath God as narrow and limited.... In all this my heart rejoiced that nothing can be compared to this infinite God and I said over and over: Lord, who is like you? My spirit, impassioned by all these sights, sang praises appropriate to what it saw. In that vision of beauty, it sang of beauty; in the sight of grandeur, it sang of grandeur; in the sight of power, it sang of power, ending everything with these words: Lord, who is like to you? **Blessed Marie of the Incarnation**

Our Lady's love is like a limpid stream that has its source in the Eternal Fountains, quenches the thirst of all, can never be drained, and ever flows back to its Source. **Blessed Margaret Bourgeoys**

I am a prisoner too—with all this wide and beautiful creation before me the restless soul longs to enjoy its liberty and rest beyond its bound. When the Father calls his child how readily will he be obeyed. **St. Elizabeth Seton**

Who except God can give you peace? Has the world ever been able to satisfy the heart? **St. Gerard Majella**

Before one has completely emptied one's heart, one exists in a state of indefinable uneasiness, and when the void has been well made one still suffers much; but there is joy in this suffering because one sees only God and desires him alone. **Blessed Eugénie Smet**

I have been made for Heaven and Heaven for me.

St. Joseph Cafasso

Sometimes, when I read spiritual treatises... my poor little mind soon grows weary, I close the learned book which leaves my head splitting and my heart parched, and I take the Holy Scriptures. Then all seems luminous, a single word opens up infinite horizons to my soul. **St. Thérèse of Lisieux**

I travel, work, suffer my weak health, meet with a thousand difficulties, but all these are nothing, for this world is so small. To me, space is an imperceptible object, as I am accustomed to dwell in eternity. **St. Frances Cabrini**

O God... you gave me a disgust for vice and shame. I did evil, but I never approved of it or loved it. You made me experience a melancholy emptiness, a sadness that I never felt at other times. **Venerable Charles de Foucauld**

I was meditating devoutly on God, when all of a sudden I saw a vast tableau of very vivid light, growing brighter and brighter at its center. A white light! And most surprising, above this ocean, this abyss of light with its thousand rays of gold and fire, I saw a dove, an all white dove, its wings spread, covering I know not how, this whole torrent of light.

Servant of God Concepción Cabrera de Armida

I am oppressed by the uncertainty of my future, but I cherish the lively hope of seeing my dreams fulfilled, because the Lord cannot place thoughts and desires in a person's soul if he does not really intend to fulfill them, to gratify these longings which he alone has caused. **Servant of God Padre Pio**

"Have a good time," they said, as usual. And the comment of a soul very close to God was, "What a limited wish!" **Venerable José Escriva**

14

Fear to Courage

"FEAR NOT, WHEN YOU WALK through the waters, I am with you, I have called you by name" (Is 43:2). Many are the fears we humans suffer through—fear of illness, fear of accident, fear of failure, fear of ecological disaster, fear of a nuclear holocaust, fear of economic collapse, fear of sin, fear of death, and fear of fear itself. The saints can help us put our fears in perspective so that we will pray for the courage we need.

Our own Blessed Kateri Tekakwitha provides an example of fear overcome by courage from the Lord. Disdained by her Indian tribe as an orphan and disfigured by pock-marks, she braved still greater rejection by her conversion to the religion of the black robes (the Jesuits). Edel Quinn of our century, an unprotected single missionary of the Legion of Mary, drove in a jeep through the jungles of Africa forming women into evangelistic teams. She is about to be beatified.

✠ ✠ ✠

There is only one thing to be feared... only one trial and that is sin. I have told you this over and over again.

All the rest is beside the point, whether you talk of plots, feuds, betrayals, slanders, abuses, confiscations of property, exile, swords, open sea or universal war. Whatever they may be, they are all fugitive and perishable. They touch the mortal body but wreak no harm on the watchful soul. St. John Chrysostom

When men wish for old age for themselves, what else do they wish for but lengthened infirmity. St. Augustine

As the body must be born after completing its development in the womb, so a soul, when it has reached the limit of life in the body allotted it by God, must leave the body. St. Anthony the Great

Let us rush with joy and trepidation to the noble contest and with no fear of our enemies [the devils]. If they see our spirits cowering and trembling, they will make a more vigorous attack against us. They hesitate to grapple with a bold fighter. St. John Climacus

It shows weakness of mind to hold too much to the beaten track through fear of innovations. Times change and to keep up with them, we must modify our methods. St. Madeleine Sophie Barat

As sailors are guided by a star to the port, so are Christians guided to Heaven by Mary. St. Thomas Aquinas

Hope everything from the mercy of God. It is as boundless as His Power. St. Frances of Rome

Ah fear, abortive imp of drooping mind; self-overthrow, false friend, root of remorse... ague of valor... love's frost, the mint of lies. **Blessed Robert Southwell**

I will not mistrust [God], though I shall feel myself weakening and on the verge of being overcome with fear.... I trust he shall place his holy hand on me and in the stormy seas hold me up from drowning.

St. Thomas More

Fear is a greater evil than the evil itself. **St. Francis de Sales**

When did it ever happen that a man had confidence in God and was lost? **St. Alphonsus Liguori**

Fear nothing, [said the Virgin Mary] you shall be my true daughter and I will always be your good mother.

St. Margaret Mary Alacoque

Take shelter under our Lady's mantle, and do not fear. She will give you all you need. She is very rich, and besides is very generous with her children. She loves giving. **Blessed Raphaela Maria**

I wish that men were as resolute as women.

Blessed Anne Javouhey

Go ahead! Courage! In the spiritual life he who does not go forward goes backward. It is the same with a boat which must always go forward. If it stands still, the wind will blow it back. **Servant of God Padre Pio**

In a higher world it is otherwise, but here below to live is to change, and to be perfect is to have changed often.

Venerable John Henry Cardinal Newman

Love Our Lady. And she will obtain abundant grace for you to help you conquer in your daily struggle. And the enemy will gain nothing by those foul things that continually seem to boil and rise within you, seeking to swallow up in their perfumed corruption the high ideals, the sublime determination that Christ Himself has set in your heart. **Venerable José Escriva**

15

Greed to Simplicity

THE WORD GREED IS NOT AS COMMON today as its eu-
phemism acquisitiveness. Whatever we call it, this
vice contrasts tremendously with the gospel value of
simplicity. "Behold the lilies of the fields" (Mt 6:28).
Jesus thought that being overly concerned about acquiring material possessions was one of the greatest
obstacles to following him.

When we are happy with such spiritual gifts as love,
beauty, and goodness, we find ourselves less interested
in worldly pursuits. But then we are bombarded with
flashy ads for things we can barely afford, and the cycle
of greedy desire, over-expenditure, debt, insecurity,
plans for reform, and fresh yearning to possess still
another thing begins anew. The saints, many of whom
freely chose poverty as a way to avoid the burdens con-
nected with possessions, have much to teach us about
greed and simplicity.

We can find interesting examples in the lives of noble
men and women who used their money for good works.
St. Birgitta, one of the richest women of Sweden,

helped finance the building of a convent of nuns to pray for her sinful countrymen. The rest went for pilgrimages to Rome and the Holy Land for herself and her entourage of holy priests and relatives. Once when she ran out of funds, Jesus told her not to ask wealthy Romans for loans, but to go out and beg in the streets. She happily complied.

✠ ✠ ✠

The more a man uses moderation in his life, the more he is at peace, for he is not full of cares for many things—servants, hired labourers, and acquisition of cattle. But when we cling to such things, we become liable to vexations arising from them and are led to murmur against God. Thus our self-willed desire for many things fills us with turmoil and we wander into darkness. **St. Anthony the Great**

If you would rise, shun luxury, for luxury lowers and degrades. **St. John Chrysostom**

Happy the man who has been able to cut out the root of vices, avarice.... What do superfluous riches profit in this world when they do not assist our birth or impede our dying? We are born into this world naked, we leave without a cent, we are buried without our inheritance.

St. Ambrose

Read the words of Holy Scripture by means of deeds; and do not be expansive in words, puffing yourself up with bare theoretical ideas.

Occupations that are necessary and result from God's ordinance are inevitable, but untimely occupations should be rejected, and preference given to prayer; especially should we reject those which involve us in great expenditure and acquiring superfluous possessions. For in so far as a man limits them for the Lord's sake and cuts off their superfluous substance, he restrains his thought from distraction... he gives room for pure prayer and shows sincere faith in Christ. But if someone cannot do this through lack of faith or from some other weakness, let him at least know the truth and press forward as much as is in his power, accusing himself of infancy. **St. Mark the Ascetic**

The love of worldly possessions is a sort of birdlime [bird droppings] which entangles the soul and prevents it flying to God. **St. Augustine**

He is rich enough who is poor with Christ. **St. Jerome**

Be not anxious about what you have, but about what you are. **St. Gregory the Great**

We should be simple in our affections, intentions, actions and words; we should do what we find to do without artifice or guile. **St. Vincent de Paul**

The man of charity spreads his money about him, but the man who claims to possess both charity and money is a self-deceived fool. **St. John Climacus**

Poverty was not found in heaven. It abounded on earth, but man does not know its value. The Son of God, therefore, treasured it and came down from heaven to choose it for Himself, to make it precious to us.

St. Bernard

My will! What are you talking about? Thank God, I haven't a penny left in the world. **St. Lawrence O'Toole**

When the Blessed Father [St. Francis] saw that we had no fear of poverty, hard work, suffering, shame, or the contempt of the world, but that, instead, we regarded such things as great delights, he wrote us a form of life.

[Christ] chose to appear despised, needy, and poor in this world, so that people who were in utter poverty might become rich in him by possessing the kingdom of heaven. Rejoice and be glad. **St. Clare of Assisi**

You, who have the kingdom of heaven, are not a poor little woman, but a queen. **Blessed Jordan of Saxony**

When the devil is called the god of this world, it is not because he made it, but because we serve him with our worldliness. **St. Thomas Aquinas**

A detached man should always be looking to see what he can do without. **Blessed Henry Suso**

We can afford to lose castles, but we cannot let a day go by without attending Holy Mass. **Blessed Charles of Blois**

After a financial crisis:
[My husband] is quietly writing by my side in as perfect health as he has ever enjoyed—my chicks quiet in bed and my father smiling.... For myself, I think the greatest

happiness of this life is to be released from the cares and formalities of what is called the world. My world is my family, and all the change to me will be that I can devote myself unmolested to my treasure.

St. Elizabeth Seton

I want to die so poor that they may say that Don Bosco died without leaving a halfpenny. **St. John Bosco**

During those few days in France [in 1909, what shocked him] was the advances made by the taste for costly vanities, and their appearance among all classes of society, even among the most Christian families, together with a great lack of depth and an addiction to worldly and frivolous distractions completely out of place in times as grave as these... in no way in harmony with the Christian life.

To the rich, [those leading a communal, consecrated ascetical life] are poor, but we are not poor as Our Lord was... not as poor as St. Francis. What a beautiful and blessed and divine thing is poverty, and how repulsive it is to human beings.... Not being satisfied with what is absolutely necessary, one is obliged, in order to have extra, to have recourse to a thousand stratagems.

Venerable Charles de Foucauld

Never did material things satisfy my heart, I felt something else, very great in the depths of my heart.

Servant of God Concepción Cabrera de Armida

Don't forget it: he has much who needs least. Don't create necessities for yourself. **Venerable José Escriva**

16

Harshness to Gentleness

MANY CHRISTIANS STRUGGLE rather impressively with faults such as greediness or fearfulness but exhibit a hard attitude toward the weaknesses of others and sometimes of themselves as well.

An example would be insensitive and abrasive ways of dealing with others at work and at home, most often with those dependent on us. I, myself, am often amazed at the change in my tone of voice in the midst of some family argument when the phone rings. Wanting to impress a stranger, I abruptly go into "sweet-gear," as it were!

The mercifulness that always leads to gentleness is a prime virtue by which followers of Christ are known. Let us always temper our righteous harshness by a manner of gentle tenderness toward others' weaknesses, for we have been set free by the mercy and grace of God.

✠ ✠ ✠

Mercy is a good thing, for it makes men perfect, in that it imitates the perfect Father. Nothing graces the

Christian soul so much as mercy. St. Ambrose

A man who is deeply wounded in his heart by provocation and abuse shows thereby that deep in himself he harbors the old serpent. If he bears the blows in silence and answers with great humility, he will render this serpent weak and powerless (or will kill it altogether). But if he argues with bitterness or speaks with arrogance, he will give the serpent an added strength to pour poison into his heart and mercilessly to devour his entrails.
St. Simeon the New Theologian

Man must be lenient with his soul in his weaknesses and imperfections and suffer his failings as he suffers those of others, but he must not become idle, and must encourage himself to better things. St. Seraphim of Sarov

You should never judge sinners, you should never despise them, for you know not the judgments of God.
Blessed Angela of Foligno

Those in union with God when aware of the sins of others live in this gentle light.... Therefore they are always peaceful and calm, and nothing can scandalize them because they have done away with what causes them to take scandal, their self-will.... They find joy in everything. They do not sit in judgment on my servants or anyone else, but rejoice in every situation and every way of living they see.... Even when they see something that is clearly sinful, they do not pass judgment, but rather feel a holy and genuine compassion, praying for the sinner. St. Catherine of Siena

Whoever will proudly dispute and contradict will always stand outside the door. Christ, the master of humility, manifests his truth only to the humble and hides himself from the proud. **St. Vincent Ferrer**

Christ appeared not as a philosopher of many words or as one who disputed noisily... but in the utmost simplicity did he talk with men, showing them the way of truth in his life, his virtues, and his miracles.

Blessed Angela of Foligno

Be kind to all and severe to thyself. **St. Teresa of Avila**

If we wish to keep peace with our neighbor, we should never remind anyone of his natural defects. **St. Philip Neri**

You can win more converts with a spoonful of honey than a barrelful of vinegar. **St. Francis de Sales**

Since the goodness of God is so great that one single moment suffices to obtain and receive His grace, what assurance can we have that a man who was a sinner yesterday is so today? **St. Francis de Sales**

The better friends you are, the straighter you can talk, but while you are only on nodding terms, be slow to scold.

Take care not to frighten away by stern rigor poor sinners who are trying to lay bare the shocking state of their souls. Speak to them rather of the great mercy of God... sometimes people are helped by your telling them about your own lamentable past. **St. Francis Xavier**

Of all the sins which a human is capable, none is so easy to commit [as back-biting], none so difficult to repair. **Blessed Claude de la Colombierè**

Meekness was the method Jesus used with the apostles. He put up with their ignorance and roughness and even their infidelity. He treated sinners with a kindness and affection that caused some to be shocked, others to be scandalized, and still others to gain hope in God's mercy. Thus he bade us to be gentle and humble of heart. **St. John Bosco**

Pride makes us hate our equals because they are our equals; our inferiors from the fear that they may equal us; our superiors because they are above us.

St. John Vianney

If you want to keep peace and charity among you, let each one be willing to take blame. **Venerable Thecla Merlo**

For none of you will Christ be a judge in the harsh sense of the word; He will simply be Jesus.

To speak badly of others is to create an infection that poisons and undermines the apostolate. It runs counter to charity, means a useless expenditure of strength, and brings about the destruction of interior peace and loss of union with God. **Venerable José Escriva**

17

Idleness to Good Works

"WORK HARD, PLAY HARD," is a slogan popular in our time. The notion is that you deserve to have all the fun you can during your leisure no matter what the expense or neglect of others. You have earned that right by your devotion to your job.

By contrast, the gospel teaches us that we are stewards of the time that God gives us. Yes, even men and women in convents need some time of recreation— wholesome playfulness. But that could never mean four hours a day of the type of TV programs which cater to bad taste and the glamor of sinful sex and violence. Nor could it mean planning an early retirement devoted to say bridge or fishing with no thought for the pressing needs of the community. We are called to serve—a basic tenet of the gospel which the saints understood and spent their lives practicing.

"The harvest is plentiful but laborers are few" (Mt 9:37). These words of Jesus refer not only to vocations to the priesthood but also to the vast works of love so needed in all our parishes, not to mention wider society. Even those confined to their own homes by illness or the tending of others need never feel isolated since so much can be done for the kingdom by offering up pain in intercessory prayer, offering the myriad duties of parenthood for spiritual needs, or by using the telephone as a hot-line for reaching out to the desperate. When we read the lives of the saints we are flabbergasted by how much they accomplished. Let us ponder the wisdom that led to such fruitfulness.

✠ ✠ ✠

We admire the Creator, not only as the framer of heaven and earth, of sun and ocean... bears and lions, but also as the maker of tiny creatures: ants, gnats, flies.... So the mind that is given to Christ is equally earnest in small things as in great, knowing that an account must be given even for an idle word. **St. Jerome**

Eulogy for his mother:
While some women exalt in the management of their households and others in piety—for it is difficult to achieve both—[St. Nonna] surpassed all in both. She increased the resources of her household by her care and practical foresight.... She devoted herself to God... as one removed from household cares.

St. Gregory Nazianzen

He who divides his time between physical work and prayer subdues his body by labor and moderates its disorderly demands; and since his soul, working together with the body, at last longs for a rest, it disposes it to prayer, as to something easier, and brings it to the work of prayer with fresh strength and zeal.... He who does not like working, feeds passions by idleness and gives his desires freedom to fly to kindred objects.

St. Nilus of Sinai

When a man does his work diligently for the sake of God, it is not a distraction but a thoroughness, which pleases God. **St. Barsanuphius**

Do something good for someone you like least, today.

St. Anthony of Padua

In times of cooling and laziness, imagine in your heart those past times when you were full of zeal and solicitude in all things, even the smallest; remember your past efforts and the energy with which you opposed those who wished to obstruct your progress. These recollections will reawaken your soul from its deep sleep, will invest it anew with the fire of zeal, will raise it, as it were, from the dead and will make it engage in an ardent struggle against the devil and sin, thus returning to its former rank. **St. Isaak of Syria**

A servant is not good if she is not industrious: work-shy piety in people of our position is sham piety.

All devotion which leads to sloth is false. We must love work. **St. Zita**

Without work it is impossible to have fun.

St. Thomas Aquinas

We have a long way to get to Heaven, and as many good deeds as we do, as many prayers as we make, and as many good thoughts as we think in truth and hope and charity, so many paces do we go heavenward.

Blessed Richard Rolle

Be sober and hard-working men; avoid all vanity in dress which will exclude you from heaven.

St. Nicholas of Flue

It is most laudable in a married woman to be devout, but she must never forget that she is a housewife and sometimes she must leave God at the altar to find Him in her housekeeping. **St. Frances of Rome**

The true apostolic life consists in giving oneself no rest or repose. **St. Camillus de Lellis**

Hell is full of the talented, but Heaven of the energetic.

St. Jeanne de Chantal

If you wish to make any progress in the service of God we must begin every day of our life with new ardor.

St. Charles Borromeo

Let us love God, but with the strength of our arms, in the sweat of our brow. **St. Vincent de Paul**

Nothing seems tiresome or painful when you are working for a Master who pays well; who rewards even a cup of cold water given for love of Him. **St. Dominic Savio**

God does not ask of us the perfection of tomorrow, nor even of tonight, but only of the present moment.

Too much work is a danger for an imperfect soul... for one who loves our Lord it is an abundant harvest.

St. Madeleine Sophie Barat

The principal trap which the devil sets for the young people is idleness. This is a fatal source of all evil. Do not let there be any doubt in your mind that man is born to work, and when he does not do so he is out of his element and in great danger of offending God.

The chief thing is to take the burden on one's shoulders. As you press forward, it soon shakes down and the load is evenly distributed.

First tell the devil to rest, and then I'll rest too.

St. John Bosco

All is too little for the Lord. I am ready to do anything for Him.... We will lie down for such a long time after death that it is worthwhile to keep standing while we are alive. Let us work now; one day we will rest.

Blessed Agostina Pietrantoni

Pray, suffer, and labor for the souls in purgatory.

Blessed Eugénie Smet

Remember that the Christian life is one of action; not of speech and daydreams.

I intend that every moment of time past, present and future be employed by me and all creatures in the best way.

In heaven we shall rest. **St. Vincent Pallotti**

Miss no single opportunity of making some small sacrifice, here by a smiling look, there by a kindly word; always doing the smallest thing right and doing it all for love. **St. Thérèse of Lisieux**

Remember that nothing is small in the eyes of God. Do all that you do with love. **St. Thérèse of Lisieux**

This tying of one's life to a schedule, to a timetable, you tell me, is so monotonous! And I answer: there is monotony because there is not Love. **Venerable José Escriva**

18

Injustice to Generosity

EVERY DAY WE CAN READ IN THE newspapers about the injustices of modern life—killing of innocent babies in the womb, battering of helpless women, incest, murders by drug abusers, accidents caused by drunk drivers, workers exploited in grueling manual labor for low pay, older people eating dog food because of low income, and racial discrimination.

The Scripture tells us that "When justice is done, it is a joy to the righteous, but dismay to evildoers" (Prv 21:15). Justice is the minimum of love. Never should the Christian substitute easier works for the justice that is due to one's neighbor. One reason for the lack of justice in the world is an insecurity that seeks to hold onto possessions rather than giving generously.

One of the most famous instances of a saint righting injustices is the story of St. Nicholas. At a time when dowries were a necessity and the lack of sufficient money an excuse for selling daughters into prostitution, St. Nicholas threw gold coins into the window of a poor father just in time to save his three daughters from that sad fate. If all parishes in our times helped support unwed mothers, there would probably be fewer abortions. Many other saints fed the poor daily from their own stores. Some founded hospitals and schools for those who otherwise could never have escaped the cycle of poverty and ignorance.

✠ ✠ ✠

If everyone would take only according to his needs and would leave the surplus to the needy, no one would be rich, no one poor, no one in misery. **St. Basil**

The bread you store up belongs to the hungry; the cloak that lies in your chest belongs to the naked; the gold that you have hidden in the ground belongs to the poor. **St. Basil**

Do you want to honor Christ's body? Then do not scorn him in his nakedness, nor honor him here in the Church with silken garments while neglecting him outside where he is cold and naked. The rich man is not one who is in possession of much, but one who gives much. **St. John Chrysostom**

All riches come from iniquity, and unless one has lost, another cannot gain. Hence the common opinion seems to be very true, "the rich man is unjust, or the heir to an unjust one." Opulence is always the result of theft, if not committed by the actual possessor, then by his predecessor. **St. Jerome**

Since our house is open to all, it receives the sick of every kind and condition; the crippled, the disabled, the lepers, mutes, the insane, paralytics, those suffering from scurvy and those bearing the infirmities of old age.... We ask no payment for this from anyone, and yet Christ provides for all. St. John of God

Extend mercy toward others, so that there is no one in need whom we meet without helping. For what hope is there for us if God should withdraw his mercy from us?
St. Vincent de Paul

Be diligent in serving the poor. Love the poor. Honour them, as you would Christ himself. St. Louise de Marillac

Every good is given us by the Lord discerningly with a particular intention. Who believes this will not ruin it.
St. Mark the Ascetic

Justice being taken away, then, what are kingdoms but great robberies? For what are robberies, themselves, but little kingdoms. St. Augustine

Give to everyone that asks thee, and do not refuse for the Father's will is that we give to all from the gifts we have received. Teachings of the Twelve Apostles

When you wish to give alms but your thought brings doubt as to whether it is best not to give, test your thought and if you find that the doubt comes from avarice, give a little more than you intended.
St. Barsanuphius

The rich man who gives to the poor does not bestow alms but pays a debt.

The rule of justice is plain, namely, that a good man ought not to swerve from the truth, not to inflict any unjust loss on anyone, not to act in any way deceitfully or fraudulently.

How far, O rich, do you extend your senseless avarice? Do you intend to be the sole inhabitants of the earth? Why do you drive out the fellow sharers of nature, and claim it as for yourselves? The earth was made for all, rich and poor, in common. Why do you rich claim it as your exclusive right? St. Ambrose

Law: an ordinance of reason for the common good, made by him who has care of the community.

Man should not consider his material possession his own, but as common to all, so as to share them without hesitation when others are in need. St. Thomas Aquinas

Here, in Naples, the Christians were no better than infidels, in keeping female slaves like harlots, overburdening the male slaves with work, reviling and beating them so that in despair many committed suicide. These sins greatly angered God and the whole heavenly host, for God loves all human beings. He has created them all and has redeemed them all by His Passion on the Cross. St. Birgitta of Sweden

You will generally find that everything is defiled with usurious contracts. That those very persons have got together the greater part of their money by sheer rapine, who nevertheless assert themselves so confidently to be pure from all contagion of unjust gain. St. Francis Xavier

Truly, matters in the world are in a bad state; but if you and I begin in earnest to reform ourselves, a really good beginning will have been made. **St. Peter of Alcantara**

The superfluous riches which thou didst hoard and suffer to become rotten when thou shouldst have given them in alms to the poor, the superfluous garments which thou didst possess and preferred to be eaten by moths rather than clothing the poor, and the gold and silver which thou didst choose to see lie in idleness rather than spend on food for the poor, all these things, I say, will bear testimony against thee in the Day of Judgement. **St. Robert Bellarmine**

Make yourself a seller when you are buying, and a buyer when you are selling, and then you will sell and buy justly. **St. Francis de Sales**

Inhuman fools who let reasonable men die of hunger while they overfeed their own dogs and horses.

Blessed Claude de la Colombierè

Of what use are riches in eternity? **St. Aloysius Gonzaga**

Do not be so anxious about a house on earth when we have such a beautiful one in heaven. We are poor, but charity compels us. We must share what God gives among the poor. **St. Soledad**

In seeing or thinking of the poor, I will make sure of helping them in the way possible to me and I will make sure of feeling really compassionate for their situation in such a way as to be transformed into light for the blind, speech for the dumb, hearing for the deaf and with a soft pillow to rest their tired limbs. **St. Vincent Palloti**

Go to the most abandoned of this world and the next.

Blessed Eugénie Smet

It is little use expecting anything from the mighty ones of this world—for the most part they leave the poor in their poverty, and mean and ungenerous as they are, turn a deaf ear to the cry of those who are weak and helpless. **Blessed Placid Riccardi**

If God allows some people to pile up riches instead of making themselves poor as Jesus did, it is so that they may use what he has entrusted to them as loyal servants, in accordance with the Master's will, to do spiritual and temporal good to others. **Venerable Charles de Foucauld**

Don't fall into a vicious circle. You are thinking: when this is settled one way or another, I'll be generous with my God. Can't you see that Jesus is waiting for you to be generous without reserve, so that He can settle things far better than you imagine?

When you have finished your work, help your brother with his, assisting him, for Christ's sake, so tactfully and so naturally that no one, not even he, realizes that you are doing more than what in justice you ought. This, indeed, is virtue befitting a son of God.

Venerable José Escriva

19

Lack of Love
to Love

P LAYING AROUND WITH THE DIALS of our radios, you
would think that our era was simply oozing with
love—one song after another about the enchantment
of love. And does not our Scripture tell us that the
greatest of all virtues is love? (1 Cor 13:13).

Love is the center of all Christian spirituality, but
there are many kinds of love: passionate desire, friendship, familial affection, kindness to the needy. All of
these loves need to be transformed and purified by the
Holy Spirit so that they do not succumb to their spe-
cific pitfalls.

The passion that could become lust or wild despera-
tion for instant fulfillment, must become a steady flame
of longing for happiness in God and in those God
sends. Delight in friendship must not lead to a cliquish-
ness which excludes others. Family bonds must not
become a stranglehold. Care for neighbor must not
degenerate into a system of control and domination.

Of course, examples of the right kind of love
abound in the lives of the saints. One that touches me

especially is the report of someone who knew the famous preacher, theologian, and bishop Francis de Sales: "If God the Father is as loving as de Sales, no one should have any fear of Him." Another is the thought of Rose Hawthorne, the novelist Nathaniel Hawthorne's daughter. Although she was brought up in the refinement of so literary a household, she spent the second part of her life taking care of cancer patients with great compassion and personal concern.

❈ ❈ ❈

You shall not hate any man; but some you shall admonish, and pray for others, and still others you shall love more than your own life. **Teachings of the Twelve Apostles**

Let none of you take a merely natural attitude toward his neighbor, but love one another continually in Jesus Christ. **St. Ignatius of Antioch**

I shall indicate to you the practice, which alone makes a man firm in the good and keeps him such from beginning to end: and this is—love God with all your soul, all your heart and all your mind, and work for him alone. Then God will give you great strength and joy.... The whole yoke of God will be sweet and light for you... and in adversity, by struggling and prevailing... you will gradually become stronger and stronger and... fear evil no more. **St. Anthony the Great**

We have loved them during life, let us not abandon them until we have conducted them by our prayers into the house of the Lord. **St. Ambrose**

Nothing so despoils a man [of grace] and leads so surely to perdition than fault-finding, speaking evil and condemning one's neighbour. To condemn means saying: so and so is a liar, an adulterer, a bad-tempered man. Such a man condemns the very disposition of another's soul, passes judgment on his whole life... and this is a grievous sin.... God alone has the right to justify or condemn, for he knows the disposition of soul of every man, his strength, his tendencies and gifts....

St. Abba Dorotheus

There is a love like a small lamp, fed by oil, which goes out when the oil is ended; or like a rain-fed stream which goes dry, when rain no longer feeds it. But there is a love like a spring gushing from the earth, never to be exhausted. The first is human; the second is Divine, and has God as its source.

What is a charitable heart? It is the heart of him who burns with pity for all creation.... He looks at the creatures and his eyes are filled with tears. His heart is filled with deep compassion and limitless patience. It overflows with tenderness, and cannot bear to see or hear any evil or the least grief endured by the creature.

St. Isaak of Syria

When we are linked by the power of prayer, we, as it were, hold each other's hand as we walk side by side along a slippery path; and thus by the bounteous disposition of charity, it comes about that the harder each one leans on the other, the more firmly we are riveted together in brotherly love. **St. Gregory the Great**

Love is made manifest not merely through giving away one's possessions, but even more so by teaching the word of God and by bodily service.

He has as yet no perfect love, whose disposition towards men depends on what they are like, loving one and hating another for this or that, or sometimes loving and sometimes hating one and the same man for the same reasons.

As memory of fire does not warm the body, so faith without love does not produce the light of knowledge in the soul.

Whoever entertains in his heart any trace of hatred for anyone, regardless of what the offence may have been, is a complete stranger to the love of God.

St. Maximus the Confessor

We cannot now form an adequate idea of the capacity for love that the soul will have in the next life, nor of that which it is at present. **St. Bernard**

There is neither father nor mother nor son, nor any other person whatsoever, who can embrace the object beloved with so great a love as that wherewith God embraces the soul. **Blessed Angela of Foligno**

There is a fire of love in our hearts, in the Lord, and there you speak to me and I speak to you the whole time, in feelings of affection which no tongue could adequately express.

O Diana, what a wretched state of affairs this is.... Our love for each other is never free from pain and anxiety. You are upset and hurt because you are not permitted to see me the whole time, and I am upset because your presence is so rarely granted me. I wish we could be brought into the city of the Lord of Hosts where we shall no longer be stranded from him or from each other. **Blessed Jordan of Saxony**

Not to hurt our humble brethren is our first duty to them, but to stop there is a complete misapprehension of the intentions of Providence. We have a higher mission. God wishes that we should succor them whenever they require it. **St. Francis of Assisi**

Love him totally who gave himself totally for your love.

St. Clare of Assisi

I [God] can love you more than you can love yourself and I watch over you a thousand times more carefully than you can watch over yourself. **St. Catherine of Siena**

[Jesus] would have died as often as he could have, and love would never have let him rest until he had done it.

Blessed Julian of Norwich

If you truly want to help the soul of your neighbor, you should approach God first with all your heart. Ask him simply to fill you with charity, the greatest of all virtues; with it you can accomplish what you desire.

St. Vincent Ferrer

We must give alms. Charity wins souls and draws them to virtue. **St. Angela Merici**

Imagine thyself always to be the servant of all.

I believe that all men must have a greater affection for those women whom they see disposed to be good.

Christ has no body now on earth but yours, no hands but yours, no feet but yours; yours are the eyes through which Christ's compassion looks out at the world, yours are the feet with which he is to go about doing good, and yours are the hands with which he is to bless us now. **St. Teresa of Avila**

At the end of our life, we shall be judged by love.

St. John of the Cross

The school of Christ is the school of charity. In the last day, when the general examination takes place, there will be no question at all on the text of Aristotle, the aphorisms of Hippocrates, or the Paragraphs of Justinian. Charity will be the whole syllabus. **St. Robert Bellarmine**

Love is not loved, not known by his own creatures. O my Jesus! If I had a voice sufficiently loud and strong to be heard in every part of the world, I would cry out to make this Love known, loved and honoured by all men as the one immeasurable good. **St. Mary Magdalene dei Pazzi**

Love is a movement, effusion and advancement of the heart toward the good.

The soul cannot live without love. All depends on providing it with a worthy object.

We can never love our neighbor too much.

There is nothing small in the service of God.

St. Francis de Sales

In our neighbor, we should observe only what is good.

St. Jeanne de Chantal

Friendship is a gentle, quiet, restrained love, while love is friendship which reaches rapture and ecstasy, knows no limits, lives only in excess.... Extreme impatience is the true feature of love.... Hating delay, nothing can restrain it. In an instant it sweeps away all obstacles, overcomes all difficulties. Nothing is impossible, nothing too hard. **Blessed Claude de la Colombierè**

All my desires turned to seek all my pleasure and all my comfort in the most Blessed Sacrament of the altar.

He asked for my heart... and placed it in his adorable one, in which he showed it to me as a tiny speck consumed in this burning furnace. Then, taking it out as a burning flame shaped like a heart, he replaced it in the place from which he had taken it. **St. Margaret Mary Alacoque**

My mother [Mary] is very strange; if I bring her flowers, she says she does not want them; if I bring her cherries, she will not take them, and if I then ask her what she desires, she replies: "I desire thy heart, for I live on hearts." **St. Joseph of Cupertino**

Concerning the mission school for Indians in Canada:
People who came to visit us could not understand how we could embrace these little orphans covered only by a small greasy rag. For us all this was an unimaginable happiness.... I carry them all in my heart and try very gently through my prayers to win them for heaven.

I experienced a strong desire that the many souls who do not belong to the Church, and so many others who do belong but who are not in the state of grace would be sincerely converted. Thus would be satisfied the desire of him who gives himself to them with such love and who wishes to be their paradise and their happiness in this life in order to be so more fully and perfectly in heaven. **Blessed Marie of the Incarnation**

The most Blessed Sacrament is Christ made visible. The poor sick person is Christ again made visible.

St. Gerard Majella

Concerning her students:
You know I am as a mother encompassed by many children of different dispositions—not equally amiable or congenial, but [I am] bound to love, instruct and provide for the happiness of all, to give the example of cheerfulness, peace, resignation and consider the individual as proceeding from the same origin and tending to the same end than in the different shades of merit or demerit.

Religion does not limit the powers of the affections, for our Blessed Savior sanctifies and approves in us all the endearing ties and connections of our existence. But religion alone can bind the cord over which circumstances, time and death can have no power. Death on the contrary perfects that union which the cares, chances, or sorrows of life may have interrupted by opening the scene where all the promises, hopes and consolations we have received from our Redeemer will have their triumphant accomplishment. **St. Elizabeth Seton**

True charity means returning good for evil—always.

St. Mary Mazzarello

Happiness is to be found only in the home where God is loved and honored, where each one loves, and helps, and cares for the others. **St. Theophane Venard**

If God's word... is spoken by a priest who is filled with

the fire of charity—the fire of love of God and neighbor—it will wound vices, kill sins, convert sinners, and work wonders. **St. Anthony Mary Claret**

To become all to all. **Servant of God Mary Teresa Bonzel**

Love of our neighbor consists of three things: to desire the greater good of everyone; to do what good we can *when* we can; to bear, excuse, and hide other's faults.

St. John Vianney

Just as persons may live with one another and nonetheless be separated in heart and in thought, just so can we be separated physically and yet be closely united in heart and in soul. This is what we are experiencing, dear father.

From a letter to her mother regarding her return to the convent:
My desire in leaving you has been that I might be for every one of you whom I love, the gate of heaven.

Blessed Eugénie Smet

You can do nothing with children unless you win their confidence and love by bringing them into touch with oneself, by breaking through all the hindrances that keep them at a distance. **St. John Bosco**

We are born to love, we live to love, and we will die to love still more. **St. Joseph Cafasso**

The love of the Sacred Heart without a spirit of sacrifice is but empty illusion. **Blessed Maria Droste zu Vischering**

The heart of a Christian, who believes and feels, cannot pass by the hardships and deprivations of the poor without helping them. **Blessed Louis Guanella**

The more we love God, the more we will want to love him. **St. Joaquina**

Give me a heart as big as the universe. **St. Frances Cabrini**

Regarding her dead brothers and sisters:
Those four innocent souls that had made their way to heaven before me surely they would be sorry for their sister, sorely tried on earth.... Before long a delicious sense of peace flooded into my soul and I realized that there were people who loved me in heaven too.

St. Thérèse of Lisieux

Being a wife and a mother was never an obstacle to my spiritual life.... I have been very happy with my husband.

I accustomed my husband, an excellent man, to come home early and find everything there without having to seek elsewhere certain diversions.... I surrounded him with a multitude of attentions. When his birthday came, I gave him eighteen or twenty presents.... He always treated me most delicately and all that I did for him was but little compared with what he deserved. He helped me put the children to bed and lull them to sleep. His home and his children there was all his happiness.

I want to carry in my heart Our Holy Father, charged with the whole burden of the Church, the cardinals, the archbishops, the bishops, the parish priests, the priests, the seminarians who waver and struggle in their vocation.... I will offer up my life for them on earth and I will spend my time in heaven in their service for Your love. **Servant of God Concepción Cabrera de Armida**

In three different ways, woman can fulfill the mission of motherliness: in marriage, in the practice of a profession which values human development... and under the veil as the Spouse of Christ.

Blessed Theresia Benedicta (Edith Stein)

Don't be afraid to call Our Lord by his name, Jesus, and to tell him that you love him. **Venerable José Escriva**

20

Mediocrity to Zeal

"THE LUKEWARM I WILL spew out of my mouth" (Rv 3:16), says the Lord. In one of the strongest statements in Scripture, we are warned against being mediocre Christians, inclined to wishy-washy compromise when it comes to witnessing to our faith and putting it into practice.

How often zealous young Catholics gradually settle into a routine of attending Sunday Mass and making short, daily devotions, otherwise living much like those around them. After some years of this lifestyle, compromises with the world can become less hard to make, and the interior life can begin to grow cold.

The saints can inspire us with their total dedication to the Lord Jesus, especially the martyrs who were willing to give their very lives for the sake of the gospel.

✠ ✠ ✠

O how happy should we be, did we but take as much pain to gain heaven and please God as worldlings do to heap up riches.... They venture among thieves and robbers. At sea they expose themselves to the fury of winds and waves; they suffer shipwrecks and all perils; they attempt all, dare all, hazard all; but we in serving so great a Master for so immense a good, are afraid of every contradiction. **St. Syncletia**

You will not see anyone who is really striving after his advancement who is not given to spiritual reading, and to him who neglects it, the fact will soon be observed in his progress. **St. Athanasius**

A good man [is one] who loves God and truly knows him and gives himself no peace in doing all without exception that is pleasing to Him. But such men are rarely to be met with. **St. Antony the Great**

For it is no small thing that God is going to give to those who thus yearn; no half-efforts will get them to the goal. What God is going to give them is not something he has made; he is going to give himself.... Toil, then, to lay hold of God; yearn long for what you are going to possess forever. **St. Augustine**

I am a debtor exceedingly to God, who granted me such great grace that many peoples through me should be regenerated to God and afterwards confirmed, and the clergy should everywhere be ordained from them for a people newly come to belief. **St. Patrick**

When I think of the saints, I feel myself inflamed by tremendous yearning.
Zeal without knowledge is always less useful and

effective than regulated zeal, and very often highly dangerous. **St. Bernard**

Sanctify yourself and you will sanctify society.

St. Francis of Assisi

So long as we are still in this place of pilgrimage, so long as men's hearts are crooked and prone to sin, lazy and feeble in virtue, we need to be encouraged and roused, so that brother may be helped by brother and the eagerness of heavenly love rekindle the flame in our spirit which our everyday carelessness and tepidity tend to extinguish. **Blessed Jordan of Saxony**

Not to go along the way to God is to go back.

Perfect married life means the spiritual dedication of the parents for the benefit of their children.

St. Thomas Aquinas

The more we indulge ourselves in soft living and pamper our bodies, the more rebellious they will become against the spirit. **St. Rita of Cascia**

The degree of zeal in acquiring stature in Christ shows whether a man is an infant or a perfected man in the present world and the world to come. **St. Gregory of Sinai**

The soul... should love her neighbor with such devotion that she would lay down a thousand times, if it were possible, the life of her body for the salvation of souls, enduring pains and torments so that her neighbor may have the life of grace, and give her temporal substance for the profit and relief of his body. **St. Catherine of Siena**

God has not called his servants to a mediocre, ordinary life, but rather to the perfection of a sublime holiness.

Blessed Henry Suso

If it were given a man to see virtue's reward in the next world, he would occupy his intellect, memory and will in nothing but good works, careless of danger and fatigue.

If it were possible for me, by drawing out my blood and giving it to him to drink, to make man understand this truth [that God loves him] I would have it all drawn out for his sake. I cannot bear that man, created for so great a good, should lose it for so little.

St. Catherine of Genoa

Do now, do now, what you will wish to have done when your moment comes to die. **St. Angela Merici**

Thanks to the goodness and mercy of God, our vocation and our love for the natives [Canadian Indians] has never diminished. I carry them all in my heart and try very gently through my prayers to win them for heaven. There is always in my soul a constant desire to give my life for their salvation—should I be found worthy—and to offer myself as a continual holocaust to the Divine majesty for the safety of these poor souls.

Blessed Marie of the Incarnation

Never say to God: "Enough"; simply say, "I am ready."

Blessed Sebastian Valfre

Daily, cities hitherto deemed impregnable are captured, men launch out into unknown seas... scientists strive to achieve results vainly sought for three thousand years—yet we pretend it is impossible for us to become saints, though every day we keep the feasts of those who have achieved sanctity.

At every cost, to please God.

Blessed Claude de la Colombierè

One just soul can obtain pardon for a thousand sinners. **St. Margaret Mary Alacoque**

On beginning his mission to the California Indians:
I wish I could communicate to [my family] the great joy that fills my heart. If I could do this, then surely they would always encourage me to go forward and never turn back. Let them remember that the office of apostolic preacher, especially in its actual exercise, is the greatest calling to which they could wish me to be chosen. **Blessed Junipero Serra**

To free a man who is bodily a captive in the hands of barbarians is a noble deed, but to free a soul from the slavery of Satan is greater than to deliver all who are in corporeal slavery. **St. John Eudes**

Make up your mind to become a saint. **St. Mary Mazzarello**

I greatly desire to become a saint, that I may be able to make [others] saints and thus procure the glory of God.

St. Peter Julian Eymard

Give me the spirit you want [the children I teach] to have. **Blessed Marie Rose Durocher**

I feel a longing and a need to be a saint. I did not know it was so easy to be one, but now I see that one can be holy and happy too. I feel I simply *must* be a saint.

St. Dominic Savio

If only I could love without reluctance... without measure... without end. **Venerable Pauline-Marie Jaricot**

Blessed are they who ardently crave sanctity, for their desire shall be fulfilled. **St. Vincent Pallotti**

We must never lose sight of the fact that we are either saints or outcasts, that we must live for heaven or for hell: there is no middle path in this.

You either belong wholly to the world or wholly to God.

If people would do for God what they do for the world, what a great number of Christians would go to heaven. **St. John Vianney**

It is a form of trade, you see. I ask God for souls and pay him by giving up everything else. **St. John Bosco**

How greatly we should long for all men to be in a state of grace! In other words, we should long to see as many living tabernacles, as many bodies and souls animated by Jesus, as there are souls in the world. How greatly we should long to see souls in a state of grace doing the holiest of all possible actions. **Venerable Charles de Foucauld**

You cannot be half a saint. You must be a whole saint or no saint at all. **St. Thérèse of Lisieux**

The Church and the world have need of a new Pentecost, a second Pentecost, a priestly Pentecost, an interior Pentecost. **Servant of God Concepción Cabrera de Armida**

It is not necessary to have been well-educated, to have spent many years in college, to love the good God. It is sufficient to want to do so generously.

Blessed Brother André

With your apostle's life, wipe out the trail of filth and slime left by the corrupt sowers of hatred. And set aflame all the ways of the earth with the fire of Christ that you bear in your heart. **Venerable José Escriva**

21

Over-Attachment
to Liberation

L IBERATION IS A CATCHWORD for political causes of the
day—liberation theology and women's liberation
to name two. Some of the planks of such movements
are truly just and worthy of our support, but not the
overall vision which can make it seem as if amelioration
of earthly conditions by any means leads to lasting spiritual liberation.

The saints had a different view of liberation. True liberation comes from accepting the salvation offered by
Jesus Christ, and then living in love. On a spiritual
plane, liberation comes not through following particular prayer techniques, but from letting go of whatever
stands between ourselves and following the will of God.
After all, how well can we respond to God if we have
one hand in his and the other clutching onto some
need we deem equally or even more important?

Imagine the liberation of St. Mary Magdalene when
she exchanged slavery to passion for ardent devotion
to Jesus! Or the joy of Blessed Junipero Serra when he
was finally allowed to leave his classroom duties to fol-

low his inner call to the Franciscan missions in Mexico and California! And what of the joy of upper-class married women saints, such as St. Frances of Rome, who dropped out of the pomp and show of worldly life and spent their time ministering to the poor.

✠ ✠ ✠

What a person desires, if he worships it, is to him a god. A vice in the heart is an idol on the altar.

The immoderate long fasts of many displease me, for I have learned by experience that the ass they make too fatigued on the road seeks rest at any cost. In a long journey, strength must be supported. **St. Jerome**

Only he who casts away his garment and approaches the Lord becomes His true follower and a preacher of the most perfect doctrine. **St. Mark the Ascetic**

Regard as free not those who are free from their status, but those who are free in their life and disposition. For example, one should not call truly free people who are illustrious and rich when they are wicked and intemperate, for such men are the slaves of sensual passions. Freedom and blessedness of the soul are the result of true purity and contempt of temporal things.

St. Anthony the Great

The soul is the user, the body for use; hence the one is master, the other servant. **St. Ambrose**

If you wish to find out whether you are addicted to the passion of gluttony, you can find it out in the following manner. If food captures your thought (so that you cannot resist it) you are a glutton. If you are not possessed by it and partake freely of all kinds of food to the extent your body requires it, you are not a glutton.... Almighty God has imparted sweetness to every kind of food, and a man who receives it with thankfulness suffers no harm. But passionate attachment should always be avoided, for it does harm to the soul. **St. Barsanuphius**

If something has become deeply united with your soul, you should not only regard it as your possession in this life, but believe that it will accompany you into the life to come. If it is something good, rejoice and give thanks to God in your mind; if it is something bad, grieve and sigh, and strive to free yourself from it while you are still in the body. **St. Isaak of Syria**

As earth thrown over it extinguishes a fire burning in a stove, so worldly cares and every kind of attachment to something, however small and insignificant, destroy the warmth of the heart which was there at first.

St. Simeon the New Theologian

To her son:
Rather would I see you dead at my feet than stained with a mortal sin. **Blessed Queen Blanche of France**

God wishes not to deprive us of pleasure; but He wishes to give us pleasure in its totality; that is to say, all pleasure.... What greater pleasure is there than to find myself the one thing that I ought to be, and the whole thing that I ought to be?... There is nothing pleasurable save what is uniform with the most inmost depths of the divine nature. **Blessed Henry Suso**

If the sea were the food of love, there would be no man or woman who would not go and drown themselves in it, and if they were living far from the sea, they would have no other thought but going to it to plunge in. [God's] love is so delightful—any other pleasure seems dismal in comparison with it. It makes a man so rich that anything else would seem beggary. It makes him so light that he hardly feels the ground under his feet. His heart is so fixed on high that he can feel no distress on earth. He is most free because he is always unhampered with God. **St. Catherine of Genoa**

Every creature in the world will raise up hearts to God if we look upon it with a good eye. **St. Felix of Cantalice**

A bird can be held by a chain or by a thread, still it cannot fly. **St. John of the Cross**

One should never deny the body what is due to it, that the body itself may not hinder what is due to the soul.

I have made a contract with my body; it has promised to accept harsh treatment from me on earth and I have promised that it shall receive eternal rest in heaven.

St. Peter of Alcantara

In general, give the body rather too much food than too little. **St. Philip Neri**

The soul should treat the body as its child, correcting without hurting it.

Though it is lawful to play games, to dance, to adorn oneself, to be present at proper plays, and to feast, yet to have an affection for such things is contrary to devotion and extremely hurtful and dangerous.

St. Francis de Sales

My will had been completely moved and was now plunged into an encompassing union which lasted until the end of my prayer. The subject of my meditation was that since God is love, I should also be all love in this union; that since he is fire, being him I should burn and become fire like him; that since love is the bond of perfection, I should want no other bond.... Following these transports, I found myself in a state of great detachment from all creatures and in a perfect disposition to cling to my heavenly spouse everywhere and at all times... so that if he wished me to go to the ends of the earth, this would become my country: for since he is everywhere, all places are the same for me.

Blessed Marie of the Incarnation

How can one take so much trouble merely to please someone? To prefer man to God, a strange and unhappy slavery is that of a man who seeks to please other men.... [I vow] never to do anything nor to leave anything undone because of what people think.... It will set up in me a great interior peace.

Blessed Claude de la Colombierè

In the middle of society and amusements he shot at me such burning arrows that they pierced and burned up my heart... and the pain I felt made me feel quite overcome.... I felt as if bound and strangely pulled by ropes, so strongly that at last I was forced to follow him who called me into some secret place.

When she left home years later to enter the convent:
I felt like a slave freed from prison and chains to enter the house of her beloved... to rejoice, absolutely free, in his presence, his riches, his love.

St. Margaret Mary Alacoque

Concerning the death of a beloved child:
It would be too selfish in us to have wished her inexpressible sufferings prolonged and her secure bliss deferred for our longer possession... though in her I have lost the little friend of my heart. **St. Elizabeth Seton**

All the wealth in the world cannot be compared with the happiness of living together happily united.

St. Margaret of Youville

Not the intellect, but God;
not the will, but God;
not the soul, but God;...
not taste, but God;...
not touch, but God;
not the heart, but God;
not the body, but God;...
not food and drink, but God;
not clothing, but God;
not repose in bed, but God;...
not riches, but God;
not distinctions, but God...
God in all and always. **St. Vincent Pallotti**

In the convent we are without shoes and stockings, we shall see if we can stand it. Make certain that on the one hand we do not want to pamper anyone, but on the other hand we do not want to kill anyone either.

Venerable Mary Magdalen Bentivoglio

Laugh and play and dash about as much as you like, only be careful not to say or do anything that would be displeasing to God. **St. Mary Mazzarello**

[A saint] was once asked, while playing happily with his companions, what he would do if an angel told him that in a quarter of an hour he would die and have to appear before the judgment seat of God. The saint promptly replied that he would continue playing because I am certain these games are pleasing to God.

St. John Bosco

You know what lively passions I have, how much I need to control my imagination and all that follows from it.... Ask for me... a profound forgetfulness of all creatures and of myself, this miserable me which seeks itself everywhere.... Outwardly I seem calm enough, but inwardly a violent storm is raging in my soul and I can only say: "Lord, save me or I perish." **Blessed Eugénie Smet**

Take good care of yourself... have a good appetite. God does not want His spouses to look as though he fed them on lizards. **Blessed Rafaela Maria**

The world strove to win me over.... I recall I spent my time now and then looking through journals of fashion, and remorse flooded my soul until the day the Lord told me not to look at them any more.

Servant of God Concepción Cabrera de Armida

Your heart wavers and you clutch at an earthly support. Very good; but take care that what you grasp to stop you from falling does not become a dead weight dragging you down, a chain enslaving you. **Venerable José Escriva**

22

Pride to
Humility

H<small>E SCATTERS THE PROUD</small> in the conceit of their hearts," the Blessed Virgin proclaimed in her Magnificat. The saints teach us that humility is not some kind of false meekness, but simply perceiving the truth. God is all, and we are small creatures, dependent but wonderful because we are the children of a God of love. Pride, whether in the form of vanity, arrogance, or demonic self-exaltation is the vice that deceives us into attempting the impossible task of trying to be little gods ourselves. Such a stance alienates us from the God who wants to save us.

Here are some examples from modern life. A man who is on the bottom of the totem pole at work comes home and plays "household Hitler" each night, yelling at his wife and administering harsh punishments to his children. A new professor, resenting the humiliations she experienced in the past in having to cater to the views of others as a graduate student, now enjoys spouting her dissenting ideas to shock her students.

The saints are amazing in their willingness to endure humiliation and not become prideful themselves. St. John of the Cross, an intellectual genius and a reformer, submitted to being locked up in a monastery by members of his order who resented his leadership and being beaten as he ran through a gauntlet each night! During this time he wrote his most famous lyrical poems of ecstatic union with Christ. One founder of an order, St. Raphaela, was sent by her jealous sister to a distant convent of the order where she was introduced not as a leader but as a maid. St. Germaine de Pibrac was forced to live in the stable by her jealous step-mother. These and many other saints went on to overcome all these obstacles by their patient love.

✠ ✠ ✠

A humble and spiritually active man, when he reads the Holy Scriptures, will refer everything to himself and not to another. **St. Mark the Ascetic**

For it is part of a truly great man not merely to be equal to great things, but also to make little things great by his own power. **St. Basil**

There is something in humility that strangely exalts the heart.
The desire for fame tempts even noble minds.
There is a kind of matronly dress which may become Christian wives without affronting Christian decorum.

St. Augustine

In a eulogy for his sister:
[St. Gorgonia] was never adorned with gold or... with spiral curls.... Hers were no costly, flowing diaphanous robes, hers no brilliant and beautiful gems.... While familiar with external ornaments of women, she recognized none more precious than her own character and the splendor which lies within. **St. Gregory Nazianzen**

I was like a stone lying in the deep mire; and He that is mighty came, and in His mercy lifted me up, and verily raised me aloft and placed me on the top of the wall.
St. Patrick

When a man is filled with pride, his guardian angel, who is near him and who urges him to care for righteousness, withdraws from him. And when a man has offended this angel and the angel withdraws from him, a stranger (the spirit of darkness) draws near, and from then onwards the man ceases to care about righteousness.

A humble man is never hurried, hasty or perturbed, never has any hot or flitting thoughts, but at all times remains calm. Nothing can ever surprise, disturb or dismay him, for he suffers neither fear nor change in tribulations, neither surprise nor elation in enjoyment. All his joy and gladness are in what is pleasing to the Lord. **St. Isaak of Syria**

For the human mind is prone to pride even when not supported by power; how much more, then, does it exalt when it has that support. **St. Gregory the Great**

Neither fear of God, nor mercy, nor faith nor self-mastery, nor can any other virtue be achieved without humility.... If some affliction befalls a humble man, he immediately blames himself for deserving it and will not reproach or blame another. Thus he endures everything that may befall untroubled, without grief, with perfect calm; and so he is angered by no one and angers none. **St. Abba Dorotheus**

Humility is the only virtue no devil can imitate. If pride made demons out of angels, there is no doubt that humility could make angels out of demons.

God in his unspeakable providence has arranged that some received the holy reward of their toils even before they set to work, others while actually working, others again when the work was done, and still others at the time of their death. Let the reader ask himself which one of them was made more humble. **St. John Climacus**

A vain man suffers anguish when he sees a humble man, shedding tears, gain God's mercy and stir men to spontaneous praise.

As a flame always rises upwards, especially if the burning matter is poked and turned, so the heart of a vain man cannot become humble. As soon as you say something to him for his own good, his heart exalts itself more and more; if he is denounced and admonished, he argues heatedly; if he is praised and welcomed, he puffs himself up still more.

St. Simeon the New Theologian

When you experience humiliation, you should take it as a sure sign that some grace is in store.

Who is free from defects? He lacks everything who thinks he lacks nothing. **St. Bernard**

Our body is not made of iron. Our strength is not that of stone. Live and hope in the Lord, and let your service be according to reason. Modify your holocaust with the salt of prudence. **St. Clare of Assisi**

The spiritually self-sufficient do often fall into error and are more difficult to correct than those who have worldly self-sufficiency. Esteem yourselves, therefore, as nothing. **Blessed Angela of Foligno**

For perfection does not consist in lacerating or killing the body, but in killing our perverse self-will.

God's word to Catherine:
   You are she who is not, and I am Who Is.

St. Catherine of Siena

It is very great pleasure to [Christ] when a simple soul comes to him nakedly, plainly and unpretentiously, for he is the natural dwelling of the soul touched by the Holy Spirit. **Blessed Julian of Norwich**

Christ shines into the bottom of the humble heart; for Christ is always moved by helplessness whenever a man complains of it and lays it before Him with humility.

Blessed Jan Van Ruysbroeck

The one sole thing in myself in which I glory is that I see in myself nothing in which I can glory.

St. Catherine of Genoa

In detachment, the spirit finds quiet and repose for coveting nothing. Nothing wearies it by elation, and nothing oppresses it by dejection, because it stands in the center of its own humility. **St. John of the Cross**

One day perhaps you will see me with the public execu-
tioner behind me, whipping me, and you will say,
"Good heavens, surely it's Fr. Philip we used to think
such a good little man." St. Philip Neri

If any man marvel that God made all His creatures
such as they should always need aid of His grace, let
him know that God did it out of His double goodness.
First, to keep them from pride by causing them to per-
ceive their feebleness, and to call upon Him; and secondly, to do His creatures honor and comfort.

St. Thomas More

Raise up your heart after a fall, sweetly and gently, hum-
bling yourself before God in the knowledge of your
misery, and do not be astonished at your weakness,
since it is not surprising that weakness should be weak.

St. Francis de Sales

What was the life of Christ but a perpetual humiliation?

St. Vincent de Paul

There are some favors the Almighty does not grant
either the first, or the second, or the third time you ask
him, because he wishes you to pray for a long time and
often. He wills this delay to keep you in a state of humility and self-contempt and make you realize the value of
his graces. St. John Eudes

The gate of Heaven is very low; only the humble can
enter it. St. Elizabeth Seton

I knew nothing; I was nothing. For this reason God
picked me out. St. Catherine Labouré

Often, actually very often, God allows his greatest servants to make the most humiliating mistakes. This hum-

bles them in their own eyes and in the eyes of their fellow men. It prevents them from seeing and taking pride in the graces God bestows on them.

St. Louis Marie de Montfort

The passions represented in a theatre are [represented] in quite a different form from their reality.... On the stage it would appear that the spirit of dominion, pride, resentment, vengeance, etc., proceed from greatness of soul and the elevation of a noble mind, while a veil is thrown over the corruption of the heart. St. Elizabeth Seton

It is only by hammer blows that God manages to humble us, no matter how good our native disposition.

St. Anthony Mary Claret

Don't I realize that the Blessed Virgin chose me because I was the most ignorant? If she had found any one more ignorant than myself, she would have chosen her.

The Blessed Virgin used me like a broom. What do you do with a broom when you have finished sweeping? You put it back in its place, behind the door.

St. Bernadette

How can we feel our need of His help, or our dependence on Him, or our debt to Him, or the nature of His gift to us, unless we know ourselves.... This is why many in this age (and in every age) become infidels, heretics, schismatics, disloyal despisers of the Church.... They have never had experience of His power and love, because they have never known their own weakness and need. Venerable John Henry Cardinal Newman

The only way to make rapid progress along the path of divine love is to remain very little and put all our trust in Almighty God. That is what I have done.

An idea occurs to me and I say something that is well received by the other sisters—why shouldn't they adopt it as their own? This idea does not belong to me, it belongs to the Holy Spirit. To suppose it belongs to me would be to make the same mistake as the donkey carrying the relics, which imagined that all the reverence shown to the saint was meant for its own benefit!

St. Thérèse of Lisieux

When one is in love, one is humble, one sees oneself as very insignificant, as nothing beside one's beloved.

Venerable Charles de Foucauld

Humility, humility and always humility. Satan fears and trembles before humble souls. The Lord is willing to do great things, but on condition that we are truly humble.

Servant of God Padre Pio

Don't be discouraged if you do not see the good you do. Most of the time people are helped through obscurity, their hidden sacrifices, instead of the fervor of a clamorous Apostolate. Above all, let us try to lay aside our own ego, for this is what ruins everything.

Venerable Thecla Merlo

Drop the affectations, those silly mannerisms that only suit the flighty schoolgirl. Let your outward conduct reflect the peace and order of your soul.

The pompous and self-satisfied manner does not suit you at all: it is easily seen to be affected. Try, at least, to use it neither with God, nor with your Director, nor with your brothers: and there will be between them and you one barrier less. **Venerable José Escriva**

23

Rebellion to Obedience

T HE VIRTUE OF OBEDIENCE is seldom even mentioned in our times. It is considered by many people childish and slavish to obey even legitimate authority. If, however, obedience is necessary with regard to lesser matters such as acceptance of the authority of good police officers, how much more so with respect to God Almighty!

Because God is all-knowing, all-powerful, and all-loving, it is right that human beings should submit their minds, wills, and hearts to him. Rebellion comes from trying to set ourselves up as gods instead. The spirit of disobedience clouds the mind and leads us, as it did Satan, to pit our wills against that of the Lord. The obedience of the saints was no mindless slavery, but rather a clear-sighted understanding of the good that comes with obeying one whose truth is unchallengeable.

It is noteworthy that so free-spirited a saint as Francis of Assisi joyfully submitted his rule to the authority of the pope. He also liked to kiss the hands of priests less holy than himself, simply because these hands were responsible for the consecration of the Eucharist.

✠ ✠ ✠

Through obedience and discipline and training, man, who is created and contingent, grows into the image and likeness of the eternal God. **St. Irenaeus**

We who are slaves of Christ make our bodies serve and our minds govern, so that the flesh receives its orders and accompanies our will which is guided by Christ our maker. **St. Paulinus of Nola**

We should fulfill the commands of God with insatiable desire, ever pressing onwards towards greater achievements.

This is the definition of vice; the wrong use, in violation of the Lord's command, of what has been given us by God for a good purpose.

It is right to submit to higher authority whenever a command of God would not be violated. **St. Basil**

God, having placed good and evil in our power, has given us full freedom of choice. He does not keep back the unwilling, but embraces the willing. **St. John Chrysostom**

Self-exaltation has brought us down.... Pardon cannot be obtained except through its opposite, humility. What has brought all our afflictions upon us? Was it not pride? Man was created for every kind of enjoyment and was in the Garden of Eden. But one thing he was forbidden to do, yet he did it. You see the pride?...

Thereupon God said: man does not know how to delight in joy alone.... If he does not learn what are sorrow and labor he will not know what are joy and peace.... The very sufferings of disobedience will teach him the blessings of obedience. St. Abba Dorotheus

The whole science of the saints consists in knowing and following the will of God. St. Isidore of Seville

Obedience is a safe voyage, a sleeper's journey. Obedience is the sepulcher of the will and the resurrection of lowliness. St. John Climacus

For those who have become lazy in fulfilling the commandments and desire to banish murky obscurity, there is no better or more efficient physic [cure] than complete obedience in everything, with faith and without argument. St. Gregory of Sinai

I vow obedience to You because Your fatherly charity allures me, Your loving kindness and gentleness attract me. In observing Your will, I tie myself to you because clinging to you is lovable above everything.

St. Gertrude the Great

God's precepts are light to the loving, heavy to the fearful.

The Christian is bound to obey the authorities when their power is from God, but not otherwise.

St. Thomas Aquinas

On her deathbed, speaking to her community of Franciscan contemplatives:
And I pray, my daughters, that you behave well and

that all the work God has had me do for you be blessed. Be humble, obedient; be such women that God may always be praised through you. **St. Clare of Montefalco**

God loves obedience better than sacrifice.

Blessed Jan Van Ruysbroeck

When I eat or drink, move or stand still, speak or keep silent, sleep or wake, see, hear, or think; whether I am in church, at home, or in the street, in bad health or good, dying or not dying, at every hour and moment of my life I wish all to be in God. I wish to be unable to wish or do or think or speak anything that is not completely God's will; and the part of me which would oppose this I would wish to be turned into dust and scattered in the wind. **St. Catherine of Genoa**

Entire conformity and resignation to the divine will is truly a road on which we cannot go wrong, and it is the only road that leads us to taste and enjoy the peace which sensual and earthly men know nothing of.

St. Philip Neri

Turn yourself around like a piece of clay and say to the Lord: I am clay, and you Lord, the potter. Make of me what you will. **St. John of Avila**

Obedience is a whole burnt-offering in which the entire man, without the slightest reserve, is offered in the fire of charity to his Creator and Lord by the hands of His ministers.

Few souls understand what God would accomplish in them if they were to abandon themselves unreservedly to Him and if they were to allow his grace to mold them accordingly. **St. Ignatius Loyola**

Never be obstinate, especially in things of no moment.

Christ does not force our will, He only takes what we give Him. But He does not give Himself entirely until He sees that we yield ourselves entirely to Him.

St. Teresa of Avila

If I want only pure water, what does it matter to me whether it be brought in a vase of gold or of glass? What is it to me whether the will of God be presented to me in tribulation or consolation, since I desire and seek only the Divine will? **St. Francis de Sales**

Feed upon the will of God and drink the chalice of Jesus with your eyes shut, so that you may not see what is inside. **St. Paul of the Cross**

No sooner had I made the vow [to become a daughter of Mary] than I was cured and given a new protection by the most holy Virgin, who made herself so much mistress of my heart that looking on me as hers, she ruled me as one dedicated to her, scolding me for my faults and teaching me to do the will of my God.

St. Margaret Mary Alacoque

I will attempt day by day to break my will into little pieces. I want to do God's Holy Will, not my own.

St. Gabriel Possenti

All of us here assembled who hear the word of life continually, know it, admire it, do all but obey it.

Venerable John Henry Cardinal Newman

Today, Lord, I offer you the sacrifice of this need for action which consumes me. I shall do only that which you will permit through him you have chosen for me [as a director]. **Blessed Eugénie Smet**

Where there is no obedience, there is no virtue; where there is no virtue, there is no goodness, no love; and where there is no love there is no God: without God we do not go to Paradise. **Servant of God Padre Pio**

If obedience does not give you peace it is because you are proud. **Venerable José Escriva**

24

Resentment to
Forgiveness

T HE WHOLE WORLD WAS STUNNED some years ago at the
sight of Pope John Paul II visiting the prison cell of
his would-be assassin, Agca, and forgiving him. One
would be expected to be bitter toward an assassin wanting to murder one in cold blood for political reasons,
but John Paul II reached into the heart of Christ to
find compassion for this confused man. He did not
hold on to any bitterness or resentment.

"Forgive seventy times seven times" (Mt 18:22), the
Lord commanded. For some Christians this is the hard-
est of all the sayings of Jesus, so much do they cherish
resentments as if they were golden treasures! Many
modern religious psychologists insist that lack of forgiveness is at the root of much physical and mental illness. Like Pope John Paul II, the saints were quick to
forgive, instead of holding on to resentment.

✠ ✠ ✠

An insult is either sustained or destroyed, not by the disposition of those who insult, but in the disposition of those who bear it. St. John Chrysostom

No one heals himself by wounding another. St. Ambrose

Hate the sin, love the sinner. St. Augustine

Anything you may do to revenge yourself upon a brother who has done you an injustice will offend you during prayer. St. Nilus of Sinai

You rehearse your brother's trespasses, and forget about your own.
    When a brother assaults you:
    Do not give way to indignation lest you do something precipitate, especially in relation to a man thrown into confusion by thoughts suggested by the envious devil.... He is worthy of pity and compassion rather than anger and revenge.... Let us be tolerant to our neighbor in time of his physical and mental distress.... Pray for your brother with your whole soul and love him in Christ Jesus, our Lord. St. Barsanuphius

To pray for one's enemies in the love of Christ; to make peace with one's adversary before sundown. St. Benedict

Regarding a woman's hatred for Catherine:
My Lord, is it for this purpose that my miserable self was brought into the world: that by occasion of me, souls created in your own image should be condemned to everlasting fire? Can it possibly be your will to permit that I, who am duty bound to help my sister to eternal salvation, should instead become for her the occasion of

everlasting damnation?... I will never give over pleading with your infinite goodness until... my sister has been saved from everlasting fire. St. Catherine of Siena

A man who is well disposed toward and loves those who revile and abuse him and cause him harm, and who prays for them, in a short time attains to great achievements. St. Simeon the New Theologian

Our friends, then, are all those who unjustly afflict us with trials and ordeals, shame and injustice, sorrows and torments, martyrdom and death; we must love them greatly for we all possess eternal life because of them. St. Francis of Assisi

No more than [Christ's] love for us is broken because of our sin, does He will that our love towards ourselves and our fellow Christians be broken. Rather, He wills that we nakedly hate the sin and endlessly love the soul as God loves it. Blessed Julian of Norwich

Thou shalt die to thyself so utterly as not to go to sleep at night until thou hast sought out thy tormentor and, as far as possible, calmed his angry heart with thy sweet words and ways; for with such meek lowliness thou wilt take from him his sword and knife, and make him powerless in his ill will. Blessed Henry Suso

Pardon one another so that later on you will not remember the injury. The recollection of an injury is in itself wrong. It adds to our anger, nurtures our sin and hates what is good. It is a rusty arrow and poison for the soul. It puts all virtue to flight. St. Francis de Paola

We should love and feel compassion for those who oppose us, since they harm themselves and do us good, and adorn us with crowns of everlasting glory.

St. Anthony Zaccaria

The sooner you forgive him, the sooner he will recover from his illness. You are the person to restore him to health of soul and body. Speak to your son again.

St. Catherine dei Ricci

Would God I might suffer ten times as much that thou might go free for the blow thou hast given me. I forgive thee, and pray to God to forgive thee even as I would be forgiven. **Blessed Thomas Woodhouse**

To be criticized, denounced and despised by good men, by our own friends and relatives is a severe test of virtue. I admire the patience with which the great St. Charles Borromeo endured the public criticisms which a famous and strictly virtuous preacher directed against him more than his tolerance of all attacks from others.

St. Francis de Sales

It is indeed just that the soldiers guard and accompany the missionary; but if despite this the Indians should kill a missionary, what good are we going to obtain by waging a military campaign against them? The military will answer me by saying: "We will inflict an exemplary punishment on them so that they will not kill others." To this I reply: "Allow the murderer to live so that he can be saved." This is our purpose here.... It should be conveyed to the murderer, after some moderate punishment, that he is forgiven and thus we shall fulfill our

Christian law which commands us to forgive injury and not to seek the sinner's death, but his eternal salvation.
Blessed Junipero Serra

The saints had no hatred, no bitterness. They forgave everything. **St. John Vianney**

Regarding the boy who tried to rape her and stabbed her fourteen times when she would not submit to his designs:
I forgive Alessandro. I forgive him with all my heart; and I want him to be with me in heaven. **St. Maria Goretti**

25

Sadness
to Joy

MODERN LIFE IS SO GRIM for so many of us. Think of life in our crime-ridden inner-cities. Think of street-people hiding in doorways from marauders. Think of small children left alone in apartments all day watching television without supervision. Think of the elderly in convalescent homes, often bereft of any company, all their relatives either dead or out of touch.

We Christians, ourselves, are not always so joyful. Look at the faces around you in the parish! Scripture tells us, however, that we should: "Rejoice in the Lord always, again, I say rejoice" (Phil 4:4). We are taught to rejoice, for we have hope in the Lord that all our tears will one day be wiped away when we are one with God in eternal happiness. Not only in heaven is there joy, but also on earth as we are given foretastes of eternity in the gifts God bestows on us each day.

The saints who suffered so much are models of how to rejoice no matter what befalls us. Think of Padre Pio enduring the stigmata yet full of deep joy because of his faith, or St. Lawrence the Martyr joking with his torturers! Or Maximilian Kolbe, radiant with joy in his starvation bunker at Auschwitz!

✠ ✠ ✠

No one is really happy merely because he has what he wants, but only if he wants things he ought to want.

St. Augustine

We may always rejoice, if we will only keep our head a little raised above the flood of human things.

St. John Chrysostom

What else do worldlings think we are doing but playing about when we flee what they most desire on earth.... We are like jesters and tumblers who, with heads down and feet in the air draw all eyes to themselves. **St. Bernard**

Long and excessive sorrowing of heart for anything sensory darkens and disturbs the mind. It banishes pure prayer and tenderness from the soul and brings a painful pining of heart. **St. Simeon the New Theologian**

Let the brothers ever avoid appearing gloomy, sad, and clouded, like the hypocrites; but let one ever be found joyous in the Lord, gay, amiable, gracious, as is meet.

St. Francis of Assisi

Melancholy is the poison of devotion. When one is in tribulation, it is necessary to be more happy and more joyful because one is nearer to God. **St. Clare of Assisi**

Sorrow can be alleviated by good sleep, a bath and a glass of wine. **St. Thomas Aquinas**

See, this kingdom of God is now found within us. The grace of the Holy Spirit shines forth and warms us, and is overflowing with many and varied scents into the air around us, regales our senses with heavenly delight, as it fills our hearts with joy inexpressible. **St. Seraphim of Sarov**

Since happiness is nothing other than the enjoyment of the highest good and since the highest good is above, no one can be happy unless he rise above himself, not by an ascent of the body, but of the heart. **St. Bonaventure**

Our natural will is to have God, and the good will of God is to have us, and we may never cease willing or longing for him until we have him in the fullness of joy. [Christ] will never have his full bliss in us until we have our full bliss in him. **Blessed Julian of Norwich**

Come into my heart and fill it with thy most excellent sweetness. Inebriate my mind with the hot wine of thy sweet love, that, forgetting all evils... and having thee alone, I may be glad and rejoice in Jesus my God.
Blessed Richard Rolle

When a man reaches the desirable haven of pure Love, even if he wished and tried his best not to, he can do nothing but love and be joyful. **St. Catherine of Genoa**

The sufferings God inflicts on contemplatives are of so unbearable a kind, that, unless he sustained such souls with the manna of divine consolations, they would find their agony unbearable. **St. Teresa of Avila**

The soul of one who loves God always swims in joy, always keeps holiday, and is always in the mood for singing. **St. John of the Cross**

Nothing but sin should sadden us, and to this sorrow for sin it is necessary that holy joy should be attached.

St. Francis de Sales

What is suffered is known only to One for whose love and in whose cause it is pleasing and glorious to suffer.

St. Isaac Jogues, Martyr

Upon my word it is very pleasant to have the name of being persecuted and yet enjoy the sweetest favors, to be poor and wretched and yet to be happy, neglected and forsaken, yet cherished and most tenderly indulged by God's most favoured servants and friends.

St. Elizabeth Seton

If the world knew our happiness, it would, out of sheer envy, invade our retreats, and the times of the Fathers of the Desert would return when the solitudes were more populous than the cities. **St. Madeleine Sophie Barat**

Thou sweet Hand of God givest joy to my heart,
And grantest that in pain I play the jester's part.

Blessed Crescentia Hoess

Out of gratitude and love for Him, we should desire to be reckoned fools.

Laugh and grow strong. **St. Ignatius Loyola**

You must accept your cross; if you carry it courageously it will carry you to heaven.

God commands you to pray, but he forbids you to worry. **St. John Vianney**

Be merry, really merry. The life of a true Christian should be a perpetual jubilee, a prelude to the festivals of eternity. **St. Theophane Venard**

The heart is rich when it is content, and it is always content when its desires are fixed on God. Nothing can bring greater happiness than doing God's will for the love of God. **Blessed Brother Miguel**

The practice of virtue became attractive, and seemed to come more naturally. At first, my face often betrayed my inward struggle, but little by little sacrifice, even at the first moment, became easier. **St. Thérèse of Lisieux**

O God, how good you are to allow us to call you "Our Father."… What gratitude, what joy, what love, and above all what confidence it should inspire in me. And as you are my Father and my God, how perfectly I should always hope in you. **Venerable Charles de Foucauld**

There are priceless moments during which I feel—a strange phenomenon—as it were a joy at the heart of suffering. My soul tastes of delights till then unknown. Without lessening in the least, pain takes on a feeling of suavity which engenders the act of abandonment to the divine will and happiness in pleasing him.
Servant of God Concepción Cabrera de Armida

If love, even human love, gives so much consolation here, what will love not be in heaven? **Venerable José Escriva**

26

Self-Hate to Self-Love

LOVE YOUR NEIGHBOR AS *YOURSELF* is God's command. Some psychologists claim that this is precisely what we do. We love our neighbor as little as we love ourselves, attributing to them all the rotten elements we know to be secretly part of our own lives! There is much confusion about the supposed Christian value of self-hate. Many passages from the writings of the saints suggest that only through the despising of self can we come to truly love God.

A closer look at such sayings in the context of the whole of genuine spirituality, however, suggests another conclusion. Disgust with one's vices, not to mention dismay at natural deficiencies, is never supposed to lead to the type of corrosive self-hatred that denies our great worth as children of God. Weak and foolish and even vicious, we are yet beloved by a God who longs to forgive us and who thought us to be of such value that he was eager to die for us.

A wonderful example of self-love is to be found in the story of St. John Vianney, so often quoted in this book. A poor scholar, it was thought that he could never become a priest. Humiliated over and over again in his examinations, he was finally let through, only to be placed in the most woe-begone diocese that could be found in rural France. At first, most of his anti-clerical parishioners ridiculed their new parish priest, the Curé d'Ars. But John Vianney's sense of his own worth as a redeemed child of God overcame all feelings of deficiency. With unbelievable zeal he spent his time, night and day in the confessional, freezing in winter and broiling in summer, hearing the confessions not only of the people of Ars but also of thousands who flocked to him from all over France. Through his prophetic gifts, he was able to read their hardened hearts and console them with his conviction that God could save them in spite of everything.

✠ ✠ ✠

For our leader, the Divine Word, does not demand a strong body and beautiful countenance, or high and noble birth, but a pure soul, well-grounded in holiness.
St. Justin Martyr

He who can love himself, loves all men. **St. Anthony of Egypt**

Whether a man wearies himself senselessly or is treated severely by his spiritual father, the heart only suffers wounds. He is struck—it hurts—but no good comes of it. It is like a sick man who is given a wrong medicine.
St. Mark the Ascetic

It is ours to offer what we can, His to supply what we cannot. **St. Jerome**

We make a ladder of our vices, if we trample those same vices underfoot. **St. Augustine**

And never to despair of God's mercy. **St. Benedict**

But often times if we brace ourselves with strong energy against the incitements of evil habits, we turn even those very evil habits to the account of virtue.

St. Gregory the Great

Our condition is most noble, being so beloved of the most high God that he was willing to die for our sake, which he would not have done if man had not been a most noble creature and of great worth.

Blessed Angela of Foligno

I myself [Christ] am Beauty Supreme from which all other beauty is derived. Yet so enchanting is the beauty of the souls of men that I gladly came down upon this earth and shed my Blood in order to redeem them.

St. Catherine of Siena

A man walks upright and his soul is enclosed in his body as in a beautiful purse. In time of necessity, the purse is opened and closed again, quite properly. And that it is God who does this work... for he has no contempt for what he has made. Further, he does not disdain to serve us in the simplest requirements the nature of our body demands, for love of the soul he has made in his own likeness.

For we shall see verily in Heaven, without end, that we have grievously sinned in this life, and notwithstanding this, we shall see that we were never hurt in His love, nor were less of price in His sight. For hard and marvelous is the love which may not, nor will not be broken for trespass. **Blessed Julian of Norwich**

We must not be unjust and require from ourselves what is not in ourselves.

Do not desire not to be what you are, but desire to be very well what you are. **St. Francis de Sales**

In spite of efforts to control interior bitterness and aversion toward others, the soul is desperately afraid of being deluded. It believes it has never had any solid virtue and that its passions were simply lying dormant from the time it was called to the interior life.... Whatever it thought to have received interiorly, it now feels has not come from God.... I turned to God... begging him to deliver me.... **Blessed Marie of the Incarnation**

What, then, does God look upon with pleasure and delight? It is the man who is fighting for Him against riches, against the world, hell, and himself, the man who is cheerfully carrying his cross.

St. Louis Marie de Montfort

Regarding confession:
Oh my soul, when our corrupted nature overpowers, when we are sick of ourselves, weakened on all sides, discouraged by repeated lapses, wearied with sin and sorrow, we, gently, sweetly, lay the whole account at his feet, reconciled and encouraged by his appointed representative, yet trembling and conscious of our imperfect dispositions, we draw near the sacred fountain. Scarcely the expanded heart receives its longing desire,

than wrapt in his love, covered with his righteousness, we are no longer the same. **St. Elizabeth Seton**

I have such a marvelous friend. I make myself content with God when I am not content with myself.

Blessed Brother Miguel

God—Who knows what clay He shaped us from and loves us more than a mother can her child—God, who does not lie, has told us that He will not repulse anyone who comes to Him. **Venerable Charles de Foucauld**

Walk with simplicity in the way of the Lord and do not torment your spirit. Learn to hate your faults, but to hate them calmly. **Servant of God Padre Pio**

Your involuntary falls, a child's falls, show your Father-God that He must take more care.... Each day as Our Lord picks you up from the ground, embrace Him with all your strength and lay your miserable head on His open breast so as to be made altogether "crazy" by the beating of His most lovable heart. **Venerable José Escriva**

27

Self-Reliance
to Prayer

WHEN I WAS STILL AN ATHEIST, many years ago, I recall finding the sight of Catholics kneeling to be utterly unbearable. How could they abase themselves in this way. Standing tall and being captain of one's own soul was a sort of cultural absolute. Later I was to realize how really dignified it is for a person to pray—how much greater stature we have because a perfect God takes our words so seriously.

The macho image of self-reliance has certainly not disappeared since the time of my youth. John Wayne has been replaced by such "greats" as Chuck Norris, Clint Eastwood, and Arnold Schwarzenegger. Nowadays many radical feminists also recommend being so strong in oneself as not to need anyone in any permanent way.

By contrast, Christians are characterized by willing acceptance of the status of dependents on God. We are exhorted in Scripture to pray without ceasing. "And whatever you do, in word or deed, do everything in the name of the Lord Jesus, giving thanks to God the

Father through him" (Col 3:17). Much self-reliance or activity without prayer leads to fatigue and discouragement. Worldliness leads to emptiness and ultimately to hell. Only when we continually seek renewal in God's love can we live with freedom in the Spirit.

Sometimes we can get bored by prayer because we have too narrow a view of its scope. There are many types of converse with God: petition, gratitude, contrition, praise, adoration, and many others you may discover yourself if you let the Holy Spirit move you. Brother Lawrence's *Practice of the Presence of God* is an ever popular introduction. All the saints were tireless in urging their sisters and brothers to a life of constant prayer.

✠ ✠ ✠

The Christian prays in every situation, in his walks for recreation, in his dealings with others, in silence, in reading, in all rational pursuits. **St. Clement of Alexandria**

When we stand praying... we ought to be earnest with our whole heart. Let all worldly thoughts pass away, nor let the soul at the time think on anything except the object of its prayers. **St. Cyprian**

Let every faithful man and woman when they rise from sleep at dawn before they undertake any work wash their hands and pray to God.... Pray also before thy body rests upon thy bed. **St. Hippolytus**

Our meditation in this present life should be in the praise of God; for the eternal exultation of our life hereafter will be the praise of God, and none can become fit for the future life, who hath not practiced himself for it now.

The daily prayers of the faithful make satisfaction for those daily, tiny, light faults from which this life cannot be free. **St. Augustine**

Reflect what great happiness is bestowed upon you, what glory is given to you, namely to converse in your prayers with God, to join in colloquy with Christ, and to beg for what you desire. **St. John Chrysostom**

For me, prayer means launching out of the heart toward God; a cry of grateful love from the crest of joy or the trough of despair: it is a vast, supernatural force that opens out my heart, and binds me close to Jesus.

St. Thérèse of Lisieux

Let us try to banish all worldly cares by prayer and hope. But if we cannot do so to perfection, let us confess to God our shortcomings and on no account abandon diligence in prayer. For it is better to be blamed for frequent omissions than for complete neglect.

St. Mark the Ascetic

God will not hear our prayers unless we acknowledge ourselves to be sinners. We do this when we ponder on our own sins alone, and not on those of our neighbor.

St. Moses the Ethiopian

Prayer attunes us for converse with God and, through long practice, leads us to friendship with Him; with Him whose love accepts even worthless men and is not ashamed to enter into friendship with them, so long as the love that lives in them gives them daring.

St. Nilus of Sinai

In a single day I have prayed as many as a hundred times, and in the night almost as often. **St. Patrick**

A man who prays without ceasing, if he achieves something, knows why he achieved it, and can take no pride in it.... for he cannot attribute it to his own powers, but attributes all his achievements to God, always renders thanks to him and constantly calls upon him, trembling lest he be deprived of help. **St. Abba Dorotheus**

If you pile up on one side of the scales all the rest of spiritual efforts and practices, and on the other— silence, you will find that the latter outweighs them all. Many are the counsels that men have; but if a man embraces silence, superfluous for him will be the work of keeping to them and superfluous will prove his former practices; he will prove to have surpassed these activities; for he has neared perfection.

When you face God in prayer, become in your thought like a speechless babe. **St. Isaak of Syria**

All the ways of this world are as fickle and unstable as a sudden storm at sea. **St. Bede**

Prayer is a wine which makes glad the heart of man.

St. Bernard

Prayer reveals to souls the vanity of earthly goods and pleasures. It fills them with light, strength and consolation, and gives them a foretaste of the calm bliss of our heavenly home. **St. Rose of Viterbo**

Praised be You, my Lord, with all your creatures,
especially Sir Brother Sun,
Who is the day and through whom
You give us light
And he is beautiful and radiant with
great splendor....
Praised be You, my Lord, through Sister Moon and
the stars,
in heaven You formed them clear and precious and
beautiful....
Praised be You, my Lord, through Sister Water,
which is very useful and humble and precious and
chaste.
Praised be You, my Lord, through Brother Fire,
through whom You light the night
and he is beautiful and playful and robust and
strong....
Praised be You, my Lord, through our
Sister Bodily Death,
from whom no man can escape....   **St. Francis of Assisi**

Worldly people often purchase hell at a very dear price
by sacrificing themselves to please the world.

Blessed Henry Suso

It is our Lord's will that our prayers and our trust
should be equally far-reaching as our prayer. For if our
trust is not as far-reaching as our prayer, we do not give
complete honor to our Lord in our prayer, and we
waste time and cause ourselves pain.

Blessed Julian of Norwich

During eight and twenty years of prayer, I spent more
than eighteen in the strife and contention which arose

out of my attempts to reconcile God and the world.

St. Teresa of Avila

When we pray, the voice of the heart must be heard more than the proceedings from the mouth.

St. Bonaventure

Approaching my burning lips to your most gentle heart, I dared quench my thirst at this divine source.

St. Peter Canisius

The great method of prayer is to have none. If in going to prayer one can form in oneself a pure capacity for receiving the spirit of God, that will suffice for all method.

St. Jeanne de Chantal

The air which we breathe, the bread which we eat, the heart which throbs in our bosoms, are not more necessary for man that he may live as a human being, than is prayer for the Christian that he may live as a Christian.

St. John Eudes

He who does not give up prayer cannot possibly continue to offend God habitually. Either he will give up prayer, or he will stop sinning. St. Alphonsus Liguori

Is it nothing to sleep secure under his guardian wing— to awake to brightness of the glorious sun with renewed strength and renewed blessings—to be blessed with the power of instant communion with the Father of our spirits—the sense of his presence—the influences of his love? To be assured of that love is enough to tie us faithfully to him and while we have fidelity to him all the surrounding cares and contradictions of this life are but cords of mercy to bind us faster to him who will hereafter make even their remembrance vanish in the reality of our eternal felicity. **St. Elizabeth Seton**

The more we pray, the more we wish to pray. Like a fish which at first swims on the surface of the water, and afterwards plunges down, and is always going deeper; the soul plunges, dives, and loses itself in the sweetness of conversing with God. **St. John Vianney**

The whole world is asleep, and God, so full of goodness, so great, so worthy of all praise, no one is thinking of him! See, nature praises him, and man... who ought to praise him, sleeps! Let us go and wake up the universe... and sing his praises. **Blessed Mariam Baouardy**

Day and night I am pursued by the same thought: one does not pray enough for the dead. Eighty thousand people in this nation die every day. **Blessed Eugénie Smet**

I know that soldiers have a lot to endure, and to endure in silence. If upon rising they would only take the trouble to say to our Lord every morning this tiny phrase, "My God, I desire to do and to endure everything today for love of Thee," what glory they would heap up for eternity. **St. Bernadette**

The wretched state of created things cannot blot out the profound joy in my soul, that "influx of peace" born of the thought of the infinite, vast, immutable beatitude of the Creator. We must "give thanks to him for his great glory" rejoicing that he is God.

Venerable Charles de Foucauld

[A soul which] remains like a lyre under the mysterious touch of the Holy Spirit so that he may draw from it divine harmonies, knows that suffering is a string that produces still more beautiful sounds, so it loves to see this string on its instrument that it may more delightfully move the heart of God. **St. Elizabeth of the Trinity**

It is such a joy when I awaken to salute God by singing.

Blessed Teresa of the Andes

We must pray without tiring, for the salvation of mankind does not depend on material success; nor on sciences that cloud the intellect. Neither does it depend on arms and human industries, but on Jesus alone.

St. Frances Cabrini

You go to pray: to become a bonfire, a living flame, giving heart and light. **Venerable José Escriva**

28

Sin to Repentance

THE WORD "SIN" HAS FALLEN INTO DISFAVOR. Some Christians are so psychologized as to imagine that they only have wounds from the past, no sins committed by their own free will. It is forgotten that sins come in the guise of very attractive pleasures, so that it does not require some terrible trauma of youth to want to lie, cheat, steal, or lust. One of the worst aspects of sin is that it hardens the heart against God.

But God tells us that His mercy is infinite. "Love covers a multitude of sins" (1 Pt 4:8). No matter what terrible sin any person commits, he or she must never despair of God's forgiveness and mercy. In repentance, preferably through the Sacrament of Reconciliation, we bring our sins to God and let him heal us. It is helpful to realize that among the saints can be found prostitutes such as Mary Magdalene, Mary of Egypt, and Mary of Edessa, and thugs such as Moses the Ethiopian. If they could repent and become holy, why not we?

✠ ✠ ✠

To him who still remains in this world, no repentance is too late. The approach to God's mercy is open.

St. Cyprian

Our turning aside from the way is not a loss to us only, but a weariness for the angels and for all the saints in Christ Jesus. Our humiliation gives grief to them all, and our salvation gives joy and refreshment to them all.

St. Anthony of Egypt

Those who have sinned must not despair. Let that never be. For we are condemned not for the multitude of evils but because we do not want to repent and learn the miracles of Christ. St. Mark the Ascetic

Let this my body, which was the instrument of so many sins, undergo every torment [of martyrdom]. St. Afra

Evil clings to our nature like rust to iron, or dirt to the body. But as rust is not produced by the iron-worker nor dirt by the parent, so also evil is not produced by God. He gave man conscience and reason to avoid all evil, knowing that it is harmful and prepares torment for him. So pay strict attention and when you meet some man possessed by power and wealth, be in no way beguiled by the demon to pander to him. But let death immediately stand before your eyes; and you will never desire anything bad or worldly. St. Anthony the Great

Sin is a fearful evil, but easy to cure for him who by repentance puts it from him. St. Cyril of Jerusalem

Everyone who commits sin is the slave of sin.
    If, whenever Christ's blood is shed, it is shed for the

forgiveness of sins, I, who sin often, should receive it often. I need a frequent remedy.

The sinner is not cast out, he casts himself out.

We avoid the eyes of men, and in God's presence we commit sin. **St. Ambrose**

Sin is nothing else than to neglect eternal things and seek after temporal things.

My sin was all the more incurable because... I would rather have You, God Almighty, vanquished in me to my destruction than myself vanquished by You for my salvation. **St. Augustine**

All hope consists in Confession. Believe it firmly. Do not doubt, do not hesitate, never despair of the mercy of God. Hope and have confidence in confession.

St. Isidore of Seville

Repentance is returning from the unnatural to the natural state, from the devil to God, through discipline and effort. **St. John of Damascus**

The more a man descends into the depths of humility and condemns himself as one not worthy of salvation, the more he mourns and sheds streams of tears. The more he mourns and sheds tears, the more spiritual joy flows into his heart, and with it flows increasing hope which gives him the most complete certainty of salvation. **St. Simeon the New Theologian**

O sinner, whoever you are—grown old in sin, imbedded in wickedness, despair not.... To encourage you to greater confidence, [God] has provided you with a mediatrix, who, by her prayers obtains whatever she wills. Go, then, have recourse to Mary, and you will be saved. **St. Bernard**

The Crucified One spoke to me and said:
"When these my sons, who through sin have departed from my kingdom and made themselves sons of the devil, do return to the Father, he has great joy in them and shows them his exceeding great delight in their return because of the pity which he has on their wretchedness." **Blessed Angela of Foligno**

You should permit yourself to be tormented by every kind of martyrdom before you allow yourself to commit a mortal sin. **St. Louis IX (King of France)**

Hide nothing from your confessor.... A sick man can be cured only by revealing his wounds.

St. Margaret of Cortona

There is no sinner in the world, however much he may be at enmity with God, who does not return to him and recover his grace, if he has recourse to [Mary] and asks her assistance. **St. Birgitta of Sweden**

To sin is human, but to persist in sin is devilish.

St. Catherine of Siena

Fire, darkness, worm, hell correspond to passions—lusts of all kinds, the all-embracing darkness of ignorance, the unquenchable thirst for sensual pleasures... foretastes of the torments of hell, even now begin to torture sinners. **St. Gregory of Sinai**

Man is changeable in this life, and by frailty and being overcome… he falls into sin. In himself he is powerless and unwise, and his will is overborne. In this time he is in tempests and in sorrow and woe. The cause is blindness, for he does not see God. If he saw God continuously, he would have no mischief-making feelings and no kind of stirring or yearning that would urge him to sin. **Blessed Julian of Norwich**

No mother could snatch her child from a burning building more swiftly than God is constrained to succor a penitent soul, even though it should have committed every sin in the world a thousand times over.

Blessed Henry Suso

When the soul is in sin, God does not cease to urge and inwardly call it. And if it responds to his gentle wooings, he receives it back into his grace with the same pure love as before, and has no wish to remember that he has ever been offended, and never ceases to show it all the benefits he can.

What a task it is to purge a soul here below and restore her with no further purgatory to her pristine purity…. She must pass through many cruel sufferings that she may gain merit by many and grievous penances. **St. Catherine of Genoa**

Even if you are committing mortal sins, keep on praying, and I guarantee you that you will reach the harbor of salvation. **St. Teresa of Avila**

No force can prevail with a father like the tears of his child, nor is there anything which so moves God to grant us, not justice, but mercy, as our sorrow and self-accusation. St. John of Avila

Just as water extinguishes a fire, so love wipes away sin.
St. John of God

Where sin was hatched, let tears now wash the nest.
Blessed Robert Southwell

Should we fall in a sin, let us humble ourselves sorrowfully in his presence, and then, with an act of unbounded confidence, let us throw ourselves into the ocean of his goodness, where every failing will be cancelled and anxiety turned into love. St. Paul of the Cross

It is human to fall, but angelic to rise again.
St. Mary Euphrasia Pelletier

Do not imitate those who deceive themselves by saying: "I will sin and then go to confession." How do you know that you will have time to make your confession? Is it not madness to wound oneself, in the hope that a doctor will be found to heal the wound? St. John Bosco

Heaven is filled with converted sinners of all kinds and there is room for more. St. Joseph Cafasso

Concerning the eternal destiny of a man who had committed suicide:
Between the bridge and the river, he repented and was forgiven. St. John Vianney

The Church holds that it were better for the sun and moon to drop from heaven, for the earth to fail, and for all the many millions who are upon it to die of starvation in the extremest agony, as far as temporal affliction goes, than that one soul... should commit a single venial sin, or tell one willful untruth.

In proportion as we comprehend the nature of disobedience and our actual sinfulness,... we feel what is the blessing of the removal of sin, redemption, pardon, sanctification, which are otherwise mere words.

Venerable John Henry Cardinal Newman

If the greatest sinner on earth should repent at the moment of death, and draw his last breath in an act of love, neither the many graces he has abused, nor the many sins he had committed would stand in his way. Our Lord would receive him into His mercy.

St. Thérèse of Lisieux

How many are your mercies, O God—mercies yesterday and today, and at every moment of my life, from before my birth, from before time itself began! I am plunged deep in mercies—I drown in them: they cover me, wrapping me around on every side.

Venerable Charles de Foucauld

Did a Magdalene, a Paul, a Constantine, an Augustine become mountains of ice after their conversion? Quite the contrary. We should never have had these prodigies of conversion and marvelous holiness if they had not changed the flames of human passion into volcanos of immense love of God. **St. Frances Cabrini**

With those tears, those burning, manly tears, you can purify your past and supernaturalize your present life.

Venerable José Escriva

29

Temptation to Perseverance

IN OUR DAY, WE FIND people of all ages bombarded with enticements to sin. Instant happiness is depicted in the media as coming from spending money on vanities. Being poor and on the lowest rungs of the career ladder is thought of as a fate worse than death. Sexual intercourse before marriage is shown as simply part of the dating experience. In such a moral climate, we have the most desperate need for the witness of the saints.

We need to remember that even the Lord Jesus had to endure temptation after his forty days of fasting in the desert. Demons plagued Christ's followers—most dramatically St. Anthony of Egypt in the desert, St. John Vianney, Blessed Angela of Foligno, and St. Catherine of Genoa.

Christians should not fear that temptation signifies some deep dark complicity with evil, more real than all their good intentions and inspired works of love. God allows us to undergo temptation that we may learn to cling to him while enduring trials and difficulties. The

key is how we handle temptation! The saints have much
to say about overcoming temptation and not giving way
to discouragement. They have stood the test and
received the crown of life (Jas 1:12).

❈ ❈ ❈

When sin is understood by the soul, it is hated by it like
a foul-smelling beast. But when it is not understood, it
is loved by him who does not understand it and, enslaving its lover, keeps him in captivity. And the poor miserable man does not see what can save him, and does not
even think about it; but thinking that sin adorns him,
he welcomes it gladly. **St. Anthony the Great**

In thy strife with the devil thou hast for spectators the
Angels and the Lord of Angels. **St. Ephraem**

An evil thought, for those who cast it down in themselves, is a sign of their love of God and not of sin; for
not the impact of the thought is sin, but friendly converse of the mind with it. If we have no fondness of it,
why do we linger in it? It is impossible that anything we
hate wholeheartedly should have long converse with
our heart, unless we are wickedly parties to it.

St. Mark the Ascetic

As the pilot of a vessel is tried in a storm; as the wrestler
is tried in the ring; the soldier in the battle, and the
hero in adversity: so is the Christian tried in temptation. **St. Basil**

As long as we dwell in the tabernacle of this body and are clothed in this frail flesh, we can moderate our passions, but we cannot cut them off entirely.

As soon as lust assails us, let us instantly say: "Lord, assist me, do not permit me to offend you." **St. Jerome**

As water extinguishes fire, so prayer extinguishes the heat of the passions.

And why, it is asked, are there so many snares? That we may not fly low, but seek the things that are above.

St. John Chrysostom

I do not trust myself as long as I am in this body of death.... The hostile flesh always draws me toward death, that is toward enticements unlawful to indulge in.

St. Patrick

When the sly demon, after using many devices, fails to hinder the prayer of the diligent, he desists a little; but when the man has finished his prayer, he takes his revenge. He either fires his anger and thus destroys the fair state produced by prayer, or excites an impulse toward some animal pleasure and thus mocks his mind.

St. Nilus of Sinai

Do not oppose the thoughts, which the enemy sows in you, but rather cut off all converse with them by prayer to God.

One must work not only until one sees the fruits, but until one's very end. For even ripe fruit is often destroyed by hail. **St. Isaak of Syria**

The demons either tempt us themselves or incite against us people who have no fear of God. They tempt us themselves when we go into seclusion from men, as the Lord was tempted in the wilderness. They tempt through people when we have dealings with them, again as they tempted the Lord through the Pharisees. But if we keep our eyes fixed on our example, that is, the Lord, we shall repulse them alike in each case.

St. Maximus the Confessor

The tempter, ever on the watch, wages war most violently against those whom he sees most careful to avoid sin. **St. Leo the Great**

So let us guard our conscience.... Let us not allow it to accuse us in something, nor disregard it in anything however small.... If someone begins to say, "What does it matter if I eat this scrap? What of it if I look at this or that?" then from this "What matters this, what matters that?" he will fall into a bad habit and will begin to neglect big and important things and trample down his conscience. **St. Abba Dorotheus**

Whatever good is to be attained, struggle is necessary. So do not fear temptations, but rejoice in them, for they lead to achievement. God helps and protects you.

St. Barsanuphius

When evil thoughts come into one's heart, [it is best] to dash them at once on the rock of Christ and to manifest them to one's spiritual father. **St. Benedict**

It is necessary that temptations should happen; for who shall be crowned but he that shall lawfully have fought, and how shall a man fight if there be none to attack him? St. Bernard

We cannot command our final perseverance, but must ask it from God.

To know whom to avoid is a great means of saving our souls. St. Thomas Aquinas

Close your ears to the whisperings of hell and bravely oppose its onslaughts. St. Clare of Assisi

If God did not protect me, I would be the worst woman in the world. St. Clare of Montefalco

Do not ask me to give in to this body of mine. I cannot afford it. Between me and my body there must needs be a struggle until death. St. Margaret of Cortona

They cast away the Divine seed either through downfalls or through being widowed of God by communion with the enemy concealed within them.... For a passion-loving and sin-loving soul is deprived of grace, sweeps it away and becomes widowed; hence, it becomes the abode of the passions—if not of demons—both in this world and in the next. St. Gregory of Sinai

He said not: thou shalt not be troubled—thou shalt not be tempted—thou shalt not be distressed. But he said: thou shalt not be overcome. Blessed Julian of Norwich

Unless you yield to us [the demons] we will never slacken our assaults on you until the day you die.... [reply of Catherine]: "I have made choice of suffering as the well-spring of my strength. It is no hardship for me, but rather a delight to endure for my Saviour's sake all you have been inflicting on me, and more besides, for as long as it shall please his majesty." **St. Catherine of Siena**

Sometimes, [the devil] inspires souls with an inordinate zeal for a certain virtue or some special pious exercise, so that they will be motivated in its practice by passion; or again, he permits them to become discouraged so that they will neglect everything because they are wearied and disgusted. It is necessary to overcome that one snare as well as the other. **St. Catherine of Bologna**

The thought comes to me to commit a mortal sin. I resist that thought immediately and it is conquered. If the same evil thought comes to me and I resist it and it returns again and again, but I continue to resist it until it is vanquished, the second way is more meritorious than the first.

He who remembers the presence of God is less open to other thoughts, especially bad thoughts.... In two ways the presence of God is an antidote against sin. First because God sees us, and secondly, because we see God.

St. Ignatius Loyola

Lord, beware of Philip, for he will betray you.

Humility is the safeguard of chastity. In the matter of purity, there is no greater danger than not fearing danger. When a person puts himself in an occasion, saying "I shall not fall"—it is an almost infallible sign that he will fall, and with great injury to his soul. **St. Philip Neri**

A man buys hell here with so much pain, that he might have heaven with less than one-half.

Occupy your minds with good thoughts, or the enemy will fill them with bad ones. Unoccupied, they cannot be. **St. Thomas More**

O loathe the love whose final aim is lust, moth of the mind, eclipse of reason's light; the grave of grace... the wrong of every right. In sum, an evil whose harm no tongue can tell, in which to live is death, to die is hell.

Blessed Robert Southwell

When an evil thought is presented to the mind, we must immediately endeavor to turn our thoughts to God, or to something which is indifferent. But the first rule is, instantly to invoke the names of Jesus and Mary and to continue to invoke them until the temptation ceases.

He who trusts in himself is lost. He who trusts in God can do all things. **St. Alphonsus Liguori**

You [God] held out a helping hand to pull me from the mud in which my affections had led me and my too easy nature had engulfed me. **Blessed Claude de la Colombierè**

Letter to her grown son:
Be not my dear one so unhappy as to break willfully any command of our God, or to omit your prayers on any account.... From the first moment I received you in my arms and to my breast you have been consecrated to God by me and I have never ceased to beg him to take me from this world rather than you should offend him

or dishonour your dear soul and as you know my stroke of death would be to know that you have quitted that path of virtue which alone can reunite us for ever. Separation, everything else I can bear—but that never. Your mother's heart must break if that blow falls on it.

St. Elizabeth Seton

When tempted, invoke your angel. Ignore the devil and do not be afraid of him: he trembles and flees at your guardian angel's sight. **St. John Bosco**

God is like a mother who carries a child in her arms by the edge of a precipice. While she is seeking at that time to keep him from danger, he is doing his best to get into it.

The greatest of all evils is not to be tempted, because then there are grounds for believing that the devil looks upon us as his property. **St. John Vianney**

Never… think we have a due knowledge of ourselves till we have been exposed to various kinds of temptations, and tried on every side. Integrity on one side of our character is no voucher for integrity on another. We cannot tell how we should act if brought under temptations different from those we have hitherto experienced. This thought should keep us humble. We are sinners, but we do not know how great. He alone knows who died for our sins. **Venerable John Henry Cardinal Newman**

Unless the will is set and deliberate there is no sin; neither is there if reason opposed temptation, and if the evil thoughts which present themselves are repugnant to it. **Blessed Henry Suso**

Fifteen is a most dangerous age for a young girl because it is her entrance into the tempestuous sea of the world. But now that I am fifteen years old, Jesus has command of my ship. **Blessed Teresa of the Andes**

In the moment of temptation think of the Love that awaits you in heaven: foster the virtue of hope.

Venerable José Escriva

30

Uncertainty to Wisdom

"IN EVERYTHING A PRUDENT MAN acts with knowledge, but a fool flaunts his folly" (Prv 13:16). I want to know the will of God, but how can I be sure of what it is? How many Christians have asked this question! Prudence, one of the four cardinal (key) virtues, has always been considered of great importance in following the way of the Lord.

Whereas simple *obedience* is needed in the case of choosing between evil and good, *prudent discernment* is needed in all those choices between two good paths where either one could be the will of God. To avoid self-deception, all the saints insist on the need for spiritual direction and godly wisdom. Among the saints, especially the Doctors of the Church, are counted some of the wisest men and women of all time. We would do well to heed their counsel.

✠ ✠ ✠

God guides all by the action of His grace. Therefore do not be lazy or lose heart, but call to God day and night to entreat [him] to send you help from above to teach you what to do. St. Anthony the Great

Many have gone through great feats of self-mortification and endured much labor and sweat for the sake of God; but their self-will, lack of good judgment and the fact that they do not deem it necessary to seek salutary advice from their brethren, make these labors useless and vain. St. Mark the Ascetic

When you intend to do something and see that your thought is perturbed, and if after invoking God's name it remains perturbed even by a hair's breadth, know from this that the action you mean to commit is from the evil one and refrain from committing it.

St. Barsanuphius

Those who stumble on plain ground should shrink from approaching a precipice. St. Gregory the Great

No men are more unfortunate or nearer perdition than those who have no teachers on the way of God.

St. Abba Dorotheus

Sometimes a man desires something good, but God does not help him. This happens because at times a similar desire comes from the devil and is harmful instead of useful; or because what we wish is beyond our powers, since we have not yet achieved a conformable life; or because it is alien to the form of endeavour we have accepted; or because the time has not yet come, when it can be fulfilled or begin to be fulfilled; or because we have neither knowledge nor physical strength sufficient for it; or because the present circumstances are not propitious. Yet the devil uses all his wiles to offer this activity in a favorable light, to incite us to it and thus disturb our peace of soul or cause harm to the body. So we must carefully examine even our good desires. It is best to act in all things with advice. **St. Isaak of Syria**

Read unwearyingly the precepts of the Lord and you will know what to avoid and what to pursue.

Without discretion virtue becomes vice and the natural impulses serve only to upset and wreck the personality.

Few pay attention to prudence because few possess it.

St. Bernard

Let the holy one pray, and the prudent man rule.

St. Thomas Aquinas

It is impossible to know the commandments and to do rightly unless the heart too is right. **St. Gregory of Sinai**

Let each look to himself and see what God wants of him and attend to this, leaving all else alone. **Blessed Henry Suso**

As too great care for bodily things is reprehensible, so reasonable care is to be commended to preserve health for the service of God. **St. Ignatius Loyola**

If I am distracted, Holy Communion helps me to become recollected. If opportunities are offered by each day to offend my God, I arm myself anew each day for the combat by the reception of the Eucharist. If I am in special need of light and prudence in order to discharge my burdensome duties, I draw nigh to my Saviour and seek counsel and light from him. **St. Thomas More**

Cursed be the loyalty which reaches so far as to go against the law of God.

Never do anything that you cannot do in the presence of all.

Never assert anything without first being assured of it. **St. Teresa of Avila**

One of the most excellent intentions that we can possibly have in all our actions is to do them because our Lord did them. **St. Francis de Sales**

I will imagine that my soul and body are like the two hands of a compass, and that my soul, like the stationary hand, is fixed in Jesus, who is my center, and that my body, like the moving hand, is describing a circle of assignments and obligations. **St. Anthony Mary Claret**

If something uncharitable is said in your presence, either speak in favor of the absent, or withdraw, or, if possible, stop the conversation. **St. John Vianney**

I know [Christ] dwells within me all the time, guiding me and inspiring me whenever I do or say anything. A light, of which I caught no glimmer before, comes to me at the very moment when it is needed.

St. Thérèse of Lisieux

In everything ask yourself only what the Master would have done, and do that. **Venerable Charles de Foucauld**

You must always have prudence and love. Prudence has the eyes; love has the legs. Love which has the legs would like to run to God, but its impulse to rush toward him is blind and at times might stumble, if it were not guided by prudence which has the eyes. When prudence sees that love could become unbridled, it loans its eyes to love. In this way love restrains itself and guided by prudence, acts as it should and not as it would like. **Servant of God Padre Pio**

Never make a decision without stopping to consider the matter in the presence of God. **Venerable José Escriva**

Selected Bibliography

Adels, Jill Haak, *The Wisdom of the Saints* (New York, New York: Oxford University Press, 1987).

Ball, Ann, *Modern Saints* (Rockford, Illinois: Tan Books, 1983).

Bowden, Henry Sebastian, *Mementoes of the Martyrs and Confessors of England and Wales,* edited and revised by Donald Attwater (Wheathampstead, Hertfordshire, England: Anthony Clarke Publishers, 1961).

Buehrle, Marie C., *I am on Fire: Blessed Mary of Providence* (Milwaukee, Wisconsin: The Bruce Publishing Company, 1963).

Butler's Lives of the Saints, Four Volumes, edited and revised and supplemented by Herbert J. Thurston, S.J., and Donald Attwater (Westminster, Maryland: Christian Classics, 1956).

Chapin, John ed., *The Book of Catholic Quotations* (New York, New York: Farrar, Straus and Cudahy, 1956).

Del Mastro, M.L., tran., *Julian of Norwich: Revelations of Divine Love* (Garden City, New York: Doubleday Image Books, 1977).

De Nevi, Don; De Nevi, Moholy, and Francis, Noel, *Junipero Serra* (San Francisco, California: Harper and Row Publishers, 1985).

Dorcy, Sister Mary Jean, O.P., *St. Dominic's Family* (New

...ope, Kentucky: The Martin de Porres Lay Community and Rockford, Illinois: Tan Books, 1983).

Escriva, José, *The Way* (Cork, Ireland: The Mercier Press Ltd., 1953).

Gollancz, Victor, *Man and God* (Boston, Massachusetts: Houghton Mifflin Co., 1951).

Kadloubovsky, E. and Palmer, G.E.H., trans., *Early Fathers from the Philokalia* (London, England: Faber and Faber, Ltd., 1954).

Kadloubovsky, E. and Palmer, G.E.H., trans., *Writings of the Philokalia* (London, England: Faber and Faber, Ltd., 1958).

Melville, Annabelle M., *Elizabeth Bayley Seton* (New York, New York: Charles Scribner's Sons, 1960).

Newman, John Henry, *Parochial and Plain Sermons* (San Francisco, California: Ignatius Press, 1987).

Philipon, M. M., O.P., ed., *Conchita: A Mother's Spiritual Diary* translated by Aloysius J. Owen, S.J. (Staten Island, New York: Alba House, 1978).

Seldes, George, *The Great Quotations* (New York, New York: Lyle Stuart, 1960).

Six, Jean-François ed., *The Spiritual Autobiography of Charles de Foucauld*, translated by J. Holland Smith (New York, New York: Kennedy, 1964).

The Voice of the Saints selected by Francis W. Johnston (Rockford, Illinois: Tan Books, and Publishers, 1965).

Index of Themes

Index of Saints

A

St. Abba Dorotheus 127, 156, 163, 188, 204, 212
St. Afra 194
St. Agnes 74
St. Agostina Pietrantoni 117
St. Aloysius Gonzaga 123
St. Alphonsus Liguori 31, 37, 70, 78, 88, 101, 190, 207
St. Ambrose 22, 46, 54, 84, 104, 110, 122, 126, 146, 168, 195
Blessed Brother André 33, 80, 143
St. Angela Merici 18, 69, 129, 140
Blessed Angela of Foligno 23, 56, 61, 110, 111, 128, 157, 181, 196, 201
Blessed Anne Javouhey 101
St. Anselm 86
St. Anthony Mary Claret 57, 78, 133, 159, 214
St. Anthony of Egypt 180, 194
St. Anthony of Padua 23, 56, 115
St. Anthony Zaccaria 170
St. Anthony the Great 36, 46, 67, 74, 85, 100, 104, 126, 138, 146, 194, 202, 212
St. Athanasius 138

St. Augustine 7–8, 12, 16, 17, 22, 28, 40, 45, 46, 54, 55, 60, 66, 74, 85, 91, 92, 100, 105, 121, 138, 154, 174, 181, 187, 195

B

St. Barsanuphius 13, 17, 28, 40, 67, 86, 115, 121, 147, 168, 204, 212
St. Basil 16, 36, 66, 120, 154, 162, 202
St. Bede 188
St. Benedict 67, 168, 181, 204
St. Benedict Joseph Labré 12, 62
St. Bernadette 32, 159, 191
St. Bernard 13, 22, 41, 47, 60, 68, 75, 106, 128, 139, 156, 174, 188, 196, 204, 213
St. Bernardino of Siena 56
St. Birgitta of Sweden 17, 61, 103–104, 122, 196
Blessed Queen Blanche of France 147
St. Bonaventure 75, 94, 175, 190
St. Boniface 86

C

St. Camillus de Lellis 116